Grimoire
OF THE
necronomicon

On the heels of his widely successful trilogy of works honoring H. P. Lovecraft, Donald Tyson now unveils a true grimoire of ritual magic inspired by the Cthulhu Mythos. The *Grimoire of the Necronomicon* is a practical system of ritual magic based on Lovecraft's mythology of the alien gods known as the Old Ones.

Fans of Lovecraft now have the opportunity to reliably and safely get in touch with the Old Ones and draw upon their power for spiritual and material advancement. Tyson expands upon the Old Ones' mythology and reintroduces these "monsters" in a new, magical context—explaining their true purpose for our planet. As a disciple, you choose one of the seven lords as a spiritual mentor, who will guide you toward personal transformation.

Grimoire of the Necronomicon features ritual forms and invocations for the daily and yearly rites of the Old Ones, individual rituals devoted to each of the seven major figures of the mythos, and most importantly, a grand ritual for personal attainment. The daily rituals provide an excellent system of esoteric training for individual practitioners. This grimoire also provides structure for an esoteric society—Order of the Old Ones—devoted to the group practice of this unique system of magic.

Praise for Donald Tyson's *Necronomicon*

"This exhaustively researched volume reproduces and connects the details of the mythology originally created by the eldritch author. It addresses all of Lovecraft's references to the book and its fictional protagonist/writer, Arab scholar Abdul Alhazred, 'the mysterious Necromancer of Yemen.'" —*Fangoria*

"Tyson isn't the first writer to attempt a full 'translation' of the forbidden text, but his may be the most comprehensive." —*Publishers Weekly*

"Descriptions of the lost city of R'lyeh, the ruins of Babylon, and other, stranger places blend with tales of monsters and demons, lies and truths. Occult nonfiction author Tyson remains true to Lovecraft's spirit in this tribute to a master of horror." —*Library Journal*

"Tyson sets about 'exposing the ways of the dead.' . . . Here, Lovecraft's skin-crawling nonexistent tome is lifted from the mists of fantasy and loathsomely fleshed out by Tyson, famed dealer in magic and spells and scribe of much nonfiction on magic and the occult. . . . Scholarly horror, marvelously illustrated. Or as Lovecraft, in a wild ecstasy that's quoted here, would praise it: *Ph'nglui nigliv'nafh Cthulhu R'lyeh wgab'nagl fhtagn. Id!*" —*Kirkus*

"…dreams are older than brooding Tyre, or the contemplative Sphinx, or garden-girdled Babylon."

H. P. Lovecraft

Grimoire
of the
necronomicon

Donald Tyson

Llewellyn Publications
Woodbury, Minnesota

FIRST EDITION
First Printing, 2008

Cover design by Kevin R. Brown
Edited by Tom Bilstad

Library of Congress Cataloging-in-Publication

Tyson, Donald, 1954–
Grimoire of the Necronomicon / Donald Tyson. — 1st ed.
       p.   cm.
ISBN 978-0-7387-1338-0
1. Magic—Handbooks, manuals, etc. 2. Ritual—Handbooks, manuals, etc. 3. Occultism—Handbooks, manuals, etc. I. Title.
BF1623.R6T956 2008
133.4'3—dc22

                                                                          2008022052

Llewellyn Worldwide does not participate in, endorse, or have any authority or responsibility concerning private business transactions between our authors and the public.
   All mail addressed to the author is forwarded but the publisher cannot, unless specifically instructed by the author, give out an address or phone number.
   Any Internet references contained in this work are current at publication time, but the publisher cannot guarantee that a specific location will continue to be maintained. Please refer to the publisher's website for links to authors' websites and other sources.

Llewellyn Publications
A Division of Llewellyn Worldwide, Ltd.
2143 Woodale Drive, Dept. 978-0-7387-1338-0
Woodbury, MN 55125-2989, U.S.A.
www.llewellyn.com

Printed in the United States of America

Table of Contents

Introduction

The main purpose of this grimoire is to provide a practical system of ritual magic based on the mythology of the alien gods known as the Old Ones, who are described in the fiction of H. P. Lovecraft, and appear prominently in Lovecraft's *Necronomicon*. The word "grimoire" means grammar. The ancient grimoires were copybooks in which practitioners of ritual magic preserved the mechanics of their art for the benefit of themselves and their disciples. It is in this sense that this book is a grimoire of the Old Ones. It is designed to give formal structure to what has until now been a vague collection of alien races and potent individual beings described in the writings of Lovecraft.

It may be objected that the Old Ones do not exist—that they are only fantasy beings created in the mind of a writer of horror stories. The same objection might be made about the reality of fairies, yet there are complex systems of practical rituals devoted to fairy magic and human interaction with fairies. Skeptical materialists will dismiss all forms of ceremonial magic as nonsense, but this book was not written for those who deny the reality and significance of spiritual matters. It is for those who have felt the attraction of Lovecraft's Old Ones, and who wish to work with these potent beings on a personal level.

A Dreaming Prophet

Lovecraft was a strange, mystical man. A precocious genius who was shunned and ridiculed in childhood, he suffered a nervous breakdown that forced his removal from school, and spent a large part of his early life sleeping during the day and wandering the streets and graveyards of his native Providence at night, when he could walk unseen beneath the stars. All his life he suffered persistent recurring dreams of alien landscapes and horrifying creatures. He transcribed much of what he dreamed into his short stories. He probably began writing his fiction as a way to purge himself of his nightmares and gain a measure of control over their contents by externalizing them.

Gradually over the years, his stories assumed a kind of coherent mythology that was centered around a race of invisible aliens called the Old Ones and their lord or leader, Yog-Sothoth, who controlled the gateways between dimensions of reality. Lovecraft himself jokingly referred to this mythology as his Yog-Sothery, although after his death it came to be known as the Cthulhu Mythos. Also central to Lovecraft's stories was a mysterious book titled the *Necronomicon*. Lovecraft dreamed the name of the book, as he dreamed so much of his fiction, and on numerous occasions saw the book in his dreams. It was, he asserted, a book written in the early part of the eighth century by a mad Arabian poet of Yemen named Abdul Alhazred, a book that was filled with secrets of necromancy so potent, merely to read a portion of its content was to risk insanity and death.

Lovecraft was vague about the details of his Old Ones and his *Necronomicon*. In part this was deliberate, a way to leave room for the readers of his stories to create their own mental pictures and form their own conclusions. Largely, however, it was due to the manner in which the mythos of his fiction grew from his unconscious mind during sleep, pieced together haphazardly from bits of his nightmares. Lovecraft himself did not have a coherent understanding of how the various beings of his mythological world interrelated. In his voluminous correspondence with other writers and fans of his work, he struggled to make sense of his own creations.

Although he toyed with the idea of writing out the *Necronomicon* in full, he never attempted this daunting task, but contented himself with inserting quotations from the dread book into his stories. It was left to others, myself among them, to seek to draw the *Necronomicon* forth from the astral plane, where Lovecraft glimpsed it in his dreams and set it down in cold print. All re-creations of the *Necronomicon* are only echoes of different portions of the one true book of the customs of the dead, which exists in its entirety only in the akashic records, but not in this world.

Lords of the Old Ones

Lovecraft cross-connected many of the alien races and godlike beings in his stories, causing them to interact and interrelate with each other. He described various individual creatures possessed of great knowledge and power, who were looked upon by human beings as gods. A number of these potent creatures ruled and led various alien species. Dagon was lord of the sea-dwelling Deep Ones. Cthulhu ruled his shadowy octopus-headed spawn. Yog-Sothoth seems to have been the leader of the race of invisible creatures who are most often given the name Old Ones by those who came after Lovecraft—Lovecraft himself applied the term "old ones" to several different races of beings.

In a general sense, Old Ones refer to only those who existed before the dawn of human history. It is applicable to the antediluvian giants mentioned in Genesis, the titans of Greek mythology, and the creatures of the waters of chaos that are described in the ancient lore of Sumer and so many other human cultures. The Old Ones are those who ruled the Earth in the before times, the ages prior to the modern evolution of the human race and the rise of human civilization. It was Lovecraft's contention that the Old Ones who had ruled before the coming of man would rule again. "The Old Ones were, the Old Ones are, and the Old Ones shall be." So it is written in the *Necronomicon*.

There is nothing in Lovecraft's fiction to indicate that Dagon and Yig are related, in any genetic sense, to Yog-Sothoth and the race of Old Ones, but there is nothing to positively show that they are unrelated, either. It is significant that Cthulhu is said in a portion of the *Necronomicon* quoted by Lovecraft to be the "cousin" of the Old Ones. This implies a kind of clannish bond between Cthulhu and the Old Ones, though whether it is a bond of blood or some other affiliation is not made clear by Lovecraft.

There appears to be a natural affinity between Azathoth, Nyarlathotep, and Yog-Sothoth. The link between Azathoth and Nyarlathotep is explicit in Lovecraft —Nyarlathotep is the "soul and messenger" of Azathoth, and of the mysterious blind idiot gods who dance around Azathoth. Yog-Sothoth is the gatekeeper of worlds, who opens the dimensional portals that permit travel between different realities. When the Old Ones are ritually summoned by wizards using ceremonial magic, it is Yog-Sothoth who opens the door through which they descend.

Cthulhu appears to be composed of a similar form of insubstantial flesh that makes up the Old Ones, who have bodies so unlike the matter we know on this planet that it defies the very laws of physics. Shub-Niggurath comes and goes through the gates of Yog-Sothoth, presiding over the sabbats of those witch cults that worship this goddess or god, for Shub-Niggurath expresses both sexes. In her masculine aspect she is the randy Black Goat of the sabbat. Lovecraft wrote very little to write about the composition of her physical body, but in a letter he described her as a "cloud-like entity," which may refer to her true form, as opposed to the avatar she adopts in her role as the goatish androgynous deity of the sabbat. It is stated by Lovecraft that the hybrid offspring of the Old Ones vary widely in their appearance, so it is possible that various branches of the Old Ones may be quite different in appearance from one another. It may be a characteristic of species on this planet that all members look similar, but it may not be so of the various alien strains of the Old Ones, about which we know so little.

Of the seven gods or lords that I have called lords of the Old Ones, Yig and Dagon are composed of matter that behaves in a more conventional way than the bodies of Yog-Sothoth and Cthulhu. It has been argued by some Lovecraft scholars that they are not alien to this planet, but evolved here. This may be so. Nothing in the stories of Lovecraft denies it. However, they are worshipped as gods by humanity in Lovecraft's mythos, and it is quite possible that they came to this planet across the gulf of space in the dim past, even as did Cthulhu and his spawn. It is significant that Lovecraft explicitly linked the worship of Yig with the worship of Cthulhu in one of his stories. Lovecraft gave no origin for Dagon or Yig. They are "old ones" in the general sense that they existed on the Earth long before the rise of mankind, and it seems probable to me that they must have had interaction with the alien races that in the distant past held sway over portions of this world. I strongly suspect that both are aliens, but on this matter Lovecraft was silent.

The Seven Planetary Spheres

The esoteric structure presented in this grimoire of the Old Ones does not appear in the tales of Lovecraft, where the various connections and relationships between the alien gods are vague. Practical magicians need more than this to work with, if they are to achieve results. They need a clear and precise framework of symbolism. In Western magic, astrology often supplies at least a part of this underlying structure. The ancient symbol sets of astrology divide reality into recognizable, rational categories. Among the best known are the sets of the seven planets and twelve zodiac signs. I have used these symbol sets to place the lords of the Old Ones and the blind dancing gods of chaos into their own separate spheres of influence.

This division is in harmony with the contents of my own version of the *Necronomicon*, where I set forth seven major lords of the Old Ones and linked them to the seven planetary spheres of traditional astrology. As might be expected, their natures and symbols have been given in more detail in this grimoire, to allow them to be called forth. Nothing in this grimoire contradicts the practical material presented in my *Necronomicon*, or in my novel *Alhazred*—it expands on that material and presents it in such a way that it may be ritually applied.

Those familiar with Lovecraft's fiction may raise the objection that he made no link between the Old Ones and the seven planetary spheres of traditional astrology. True enough. However, it has long been a common practice in the Western esoteric tradition to use the symbol sets of astrology to categorize various groups of esoteric beings or occult qualities. This is not a modern conceit, but goes back many centuries. It was done because it is useful, for purely practical reasons, to make this kind of symbolic association. When the lords of the Old Ones are placed on the spheres of the planets, all the occult correspondences for the planetary spheres become available to use in summoning them and directing them during ritual work.

It should be unnecessary for me to point out that we are not discussing the actual physical planetary bodies here, but the esoteric spheres of the planets, which are astral worlds. The planetary spheres represent separate realms of reality, each dominated and colored by the qualities of the ancient god from which the planet derives its name. The sphere of Mars, for example, is a realm dominated by all things martial in nature. The sphere of Venus is a realm devoted to all matters pertaining to various forms of love, both spiritual and carnal. So for the rest. By placing Cthulhu into the sphere of Mars, all the martial symbolism of this sphere can be applied ritually to invoke and petition Cthulhu and his various agents.

The Order of the Old Ones

My purpose in writing this practical grimoire was twofold—not only to provide a workable system of magic based on the lords of the Old Ones, but also to set forth the external framework for an esoteric society devoted to the group practice of this system of magic. I have dubbed this society the Order of the Old Ones. The magic in this grimoire may be worked by a solitary ritualist, but it may also be done in a group setting. The essential structure of a society devoted to ceremonial interaction with the Old Ones has been laid forth, with the hope that enterprising groups of readers may wish to make the OOO a reality.

In his stories, Lovecraft mentioned human religious cults that worship these various potent beings. The Old Ones and Yog-Sothoth were adored and propitiated by the early European settlers of New England, and by the native Indians who occupied the same land before them, in stone circles erected on hilltops. Cults in Greenland, in the swamps of Louisiana, and in the South Seas worshipped Cthulhu. Witches, or at least groups of ritual magicians who were labeled as witches by medieval chroniclers and priests, summoned and adored Nyarlathotep and Shub-Niggurath. Nyarlathotep presided over the witch sabbats as the archetypal figure known as the Black Man, and Shub-Niggurath came in the material guise of the Black Goat—she is also known in her female form as the Goat with a Thousand Young in Lovecraft's fiction.

In Lovecraft's stories, the human cults of the Old Ones are devoted to the various alien gods individually. The worshippers of Cthulhu have their own cult, for example, as do the Native American worshippers of Yig. The teachings of the Order of the Old Ones depart from this model by combining the seven great lords in a single system of magic. Each of the lords receives a day of the week that is devoted to the ritual observance and petitioning of that lord. Formal observances devoted to the blind dancing gods are done on the equinoxes of the year.

Whether or not the Order of the Old Ones described in this book is embraced by readers, and in time is made to pass from the astral reality of my imagination into the physical reality of the greater world, the daily rituals in this grimoire will provide an excellent system of esoteric training for individual practitioners. They are a way to get in touch with Lovecraft's great beings, and to draw upon their power for personal advantages both on the spiritual and material levels. For decades, attempts have been made to incorporate bits and pieces of Lovecraft's mythos into modern Western magic. It was my conviction that it deserved its own integrated system of rituals, and was important enough to stand on its own feet. Perhaps in time it will acquire its own order of dedicated practitioners.

The Work of the Trapezohedron

Central to the life of each member of the Order of the Old Ones will be the great work of personal transformation. This is linked with the great work of the Old Ones themselves, as described by Lovecraft—the elevation of the planet Earth from its fallen material state to its former more spiritual condition. I have called it the Work of the Trapezohedron, in reference to this three-dimensional geometric structure that figures so prominently in one of Lovecraft's short stories. Before the Earth can be elevated through the dimensional gateways of Yog-Sothoth by the Old Ones, it must be cleansed of its dross; similarly, the great work of members of the Order of the Old Ones involves refining the mind and training the body to achieve a higher state of being.

The great work of personal transformation is the central task of spiritual alchemy, and also of all major schools of ceremonial magic. In this grimoire it takes the form of seven paths, each represented by a lord of the Old Ones, who acts as a kind of spiritual mentor. The disciple chooses one of the lords as a personal teacher who exemplifies the higher ideals of that path of attainment. Fulfillment is marked by a pledge made on the astral level before the throne of Azathoth to serve the great work of the Old Ones, the purification and restoration of the Earth to her former spiritual glory.

The intention of the Old Ones to cleanse and elevate our world, if we take it seriously as a possible future event, may not be fulfilled for centuries, or even millennia. Perhaps it is not destined to happen in a material sense at all, but may have a more symbolic meaning that applies to the astral realms and an inner mental reality, rather than to the physical substance of this planet. Whatever its ultimate realization, it provides a model for personal spiritual transformation and perfection, and it is used in this way in this grimoire. The disciples of the Order of the Old Ones will walk seven paths to attainment, each path presided over by one of the seven lords.

Chaos Magic and the Apocalypse

This system of magic is a kind of chaos magic, and it cannot be otherwise, since Azathoth is the god of chaos and Nyarlathotep is his soul and messenger. It bears similarities with the doctrines of the Gnostics, who had as their ultimate purpose the elevation of humanity from its condition of ignorance and despair to its rightful state of spiritual enlightenment among the stars. This involved recognizing the ultimate unimportance of lower, physical matters in favor of higher, spiritual concerns.

To Christians, the religion of the Gnostics appeared Satanic. A similar uncharitable view might be taken regarding the great work of the Old Ones and those who seek to forward it in this world. The difference between an angel and a demon is often only a matter of perspective—one culture's god is another culture's devil. To those who believe that their religion is the sole true faith, all other religions are false, and all other believers are heretics.

There are aspects of the higher teaching of Aleister Crowley in his *Book of the Law* that seem at first consideration quite devilish. They shocked even Crowley himself when he recorded them, as they were dictated by his guardian angel Aiwass. Similarly, some of the statements of the Enochian angels, as delivered psychically to John Dee and Edward Kelley, have a devilish cast. Kelley was as shocked and disturbed by the instructions of the Enochian angels as Crowley was over the communications of Aiwass.

It is useful to bear in mind that in the stories of Lovecraft, the Old Ones are presented as evil monsters intent on destroying our world. However, it is possible to look behind the surface and form a quite different picture. From their own point of view, they were not trying to destroy the world but to save her from her fallen state. This involved a period of cleansing, which may be very similar to the cleansing period described in the biblical book Revelation. Crowley's Aiwass predicted a coming time of turmoil and violence, as did the Enochian angels. It is very possible that they were all talking about the same thing, and that it is evil only from a lower human perspective.

Fundamentalist Christians have come to this realization about the violent times described in Revelation—they welcome them and look forward to them, since they will mean that a select few of the chosen of God will put off their lower nature and ascend into heaven in a higher and more spiritual nature. For those with a different perspective, these end times might be regarded with horror as the destruction of the present world, or at least as the end of the present state of the world. Change is often viewed with dread, as something evil in itself.

The great work of the Old Ones may be identical to the apocalyptic vision foretold in the biblical book Revelation. It will be marked by a transformation that necessitates widespread destruction of the present existing state of the world, followed by the emergence of a more spiritual condition. In Lovecraft's fiction, those who survive the great work of the Old Ones will be those chosen by the Old Ones, who have put off their lower earthly natures and been transformed into something less tangible that approaches pure mind.

The chaotic nature of the magic of the Old Ones is represented in the rituals by circumambulation around the altar of practice in a leftward, or widdershins, direction. It is the usual practice to move around the altar in a sunwise direction during rituals. Counterclockwise circumambulation is often considered to be the mark of black magic, but it is more accurate to look upon it as a significator of chaos magic, since in general it results in the release and expansion of force, as opposed to its concentration in the center. Witches sometimes used this kind of turning in malefic spells since it liberates large amounts of raw occult energy.

The Long Chant

The Long Chant that forms so crucial a part in the personal great work of members of the Order was described by Lovecraft as necessary to invoke the Old Ones into the stone circle, but the chant was never actually given by him. Lovecraft indicated that it occupied a certain page of the English translation of the *Necronomicon* made by the great sage Dr. John Dee, who is famous in history as the advisor to Elizabeth the First, Queen of England, but is better known in occult circles as the magician who ushered the Enochian language and Enochian teachings into the world.

Unfortunately, Dee's translation of the *Necronomicon* does not exist. It was necessary to compose the Long Chant using the same kind of scrying technique that was employed by Dee's seer, the alchemist Edward Kelley, who communicated with the Enochian angels through a globe of crystal—a technique of spirit communication as old in England as Merlin. In consideration of its stated origin, I have rendered the chant into the Enochian language, which has immense potency in the invocation of spirits. It is quite possible that had Dee translated the *Necronomicon*, he would have used the Enochian tongue for the Long Chant, as a language best suited for drawing down spiritual beings. The link between the Long Chant and John Dee is not spurious but was explicitly made by Lovecraft himself.

In connection with the personal great work pursued by members of the Order of the Old Ones, the Long Chant is used to draw Nyarlathotep to the edge of the ritual stone circle, so that this lord can fulfill his function as messenger to Azathoth, and lead the disciple to the very throne of chaos itself, for the purpose of inscribing his name into the true *Necronomicon*, as a loyal follower of the Old Ones and a willing partner in their larger great work, the cleansing and elevation of the planet Earth to her former spiritual estate. This greater purpose is not unlike the higher destiny embraced by the Gnostics, who were so reviled by the Christian church in the early centuries of the present era.

It is part of the lore of European witchcraft that the apprentice witch inscribed his or her name in a great book under the watchful gaze of the Black Man of the sabbat, and received a mark from the Black Man in token of the event. Lovecraft described just such a scene in one of his stories, where Nyarlathotep presides as the Black Man of the sabbat, and the signing is held before the throne of Azathoth at the center of chaos. It is for this reason that the fulfillment of the personal great work of the disciples of the Order of the Old Ones takes place on the astral level before the throne of Azathoth, and is presided over by Nyarlathotep.

The Enochian Language

Differences of opinion exist as to the correct way to vocalize Enochian words. I have provided a phonetic version of the Long Chant that gives the pronunciation that I use in my own work. It is similar to the pronunciation used by Aleister Crowley. Consideration was given to the sonorous effect of the words when vibrated on the air, and to the rhythms of speech. It was for this reason that Crowley's practice of always pronouncing the letter z as zode was retained. Crowley was a showman and had a good sense of the emotional power of the spoken word.

The most important matter to bear in mind when pronouncing Enochian is that each letter of Enochian embodies a separate noncorporeal intelligence. Enochian words are not merely composed of letters—they are composed of spirits. It is important that none of the letters be completely silent. Unless the letter is voiced on the air, the spiritual being it represents is not invoked and actualized during the ritual. The power that being would have contributed to the success of the ritual is lost.

An error made by scholars of Dee and the Enochian language is to simplify its pronunciation. This seems like a good idea, since it makes speaking Enochian words much easier, but it fails to take into account the realities of practical magic, which these scholars usually do not understand. It is significant that many Enochian names are unpronounceable without the insertion of additional vowels. This suggests that these names, and Enochian words in general, were never intended to be pronounced like the words of common languages, but in a ritualistic manner that gives balanced attention to each individual letter.

Those who prefer to pronounce the Long Chant in another manner will easily be able to do so, since I have provided the original Enochian text below the phonetic Enochian text. It is possible to voice the Long Chant only in Enochian, or even to voice it only in English, but it is structured so that it will be most potent if the English wording of each line is spoken directly following the Enochian wording. In this way a kind of echo or response for each Enochian line is achieved, which serves to clarify the meaning of the text. If the Long Chant is worked by ritualists whose common tongue is other than English, the English text may be translated into that language, while the Enochian remains unchanged.

The Seals of the Old Ones

The seals of the seven lords of the Old Ones and of the twelve dancing gods that play so important a part in the rituals of practical magic in this grimoire were composed using my system of power glyphs, which I find to be a versitile tool for making seals of all kinds and for all purposes. The basis for the power glyphs is quite simple—the letters of the English alphabet, reduced to twenty-four by combining the I and J, and the U and V, are transformed into simple graphic shapes that possess fundamental esoteric energies. By joining these glyphs together, names and words can be represented and expressed as graphic patterns.

There are many possible ways the power glyphs can be fitted together to form the seal of a name. Which pattern is ultimately selected is a matter for intuition and meditation. Sometimes the final pattern comes easily, and other times it requires hours of manipulation as dozens of possible patterns are tried and rejected. The formation of seals is guided by several general principles. All letters in the name should be clearly expressed in the seal—two similar glyphs should not be overlapped so that one completely hides the other, for example, nor should two glyphs be joined so that they appear to represent another glyph entirely that is not among the letters of the name. The glyphs should all touch, or smaller glyphs should be contained in the centers of larger glyphs—it is not good practice to have single glyphs floating apart from the rest of the seal. The patterns should be balanced and centered. In general the glyphs should not be rotated or excessively distorted, although this is sometimes necessary to a limited degree to achieve a pleasing result.

The seals created with power glyphs are individual and unique, each an expression of the psyche of its maker. Enterprising users of this grimoire may wish to construct their own seals of the Old Ones. For this purpose I have included a chart showing the separate power glyphs. Good results should be achieved by using the seals I have provided. Each has its own resonance and unique personality. A more complete examination of the power glyphs and their use will be found in my book *Familiar Spirits* (Llewellyn, 2004).

Beyond Good and Evil

In offering this grimoire of the magic of the Old Ones for publication, I am conscious that it will be decried as Satanic in some religious quarters. This places me in excellent company. The teachings in Aleister Crowley's *Book of the Law* have been similarly characterized. So were the beliefs of the Gnostics. So were the Enochian conversations recorded by John Dee. Indeed, so were the beliefs and practices of witches in Europe, who were burned alive by the thousands during the Renaissance. The working of any magic of any kind has been condemned in the past, and in the present, as devilish by devout Christians, and by fervent religious believers of other major religions.

I do not regard the teachings in this grimoire as evil. In Lovecraft's stories, the Old Ones are presented as evil beings, but this is merely the common human reaction to their purpose, which is the restoration of this world to her former spiritual estate. It is not the intention of the Old Ones to exterminate humanity in order to cause human suffering, but rather it is a necessity of their great work of many ages that humanity either be transformed into a more spiritual condition that will not hinder the elevation of the Earth, or be removed from this planet. Since the Old Ones do not have human emotions or sympathies, they are not concerned with the survival of our race. It is a matter of indifference to them.

This does not mean, however, that humanity must perish when this work is fulfilled. If human beings are able to transform and spiritualize their own natures by achieving gnosis or enlightenment, as the great sages of past ages are reported to have done, they will no longer obstruct the work of the Old Ones, and will be elevated to a higher estate along with the purified body of the Earth. Perhaps this higher dimension of reality may be called heaven by religious believers. It may even be that this elevation of a spiritualized portion of humanity has been prophesied in the book of Revelation and other ancient prophetic texts.

The Old Ones care nothing for human beliefs and human religions. However, Lovecraft's tales indicate that it is possible for human beings to invoke them and interact with them for human purposes through the use of magic, and it is for this practical benefit that this grimoire was written. Whatever their ultimate reality, the

POWER GLYPHS

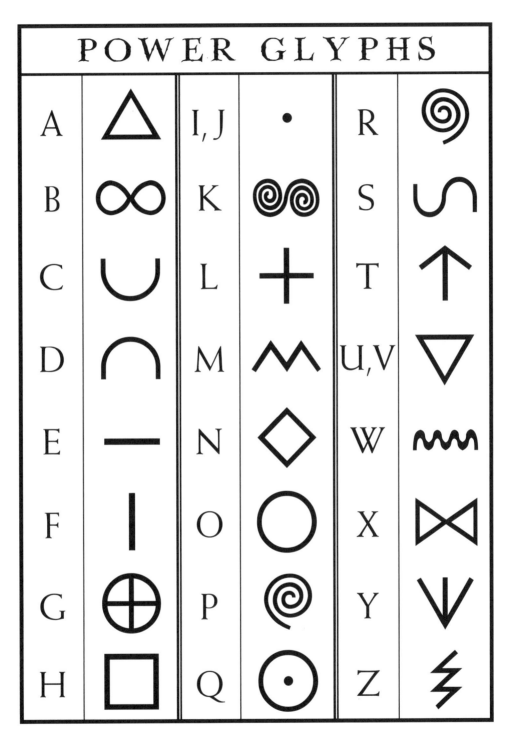

The Power Glyphs

Old Ones now have existence on the astral plane, conceived in the minds of millions of readers of Lovecraft's fiction, and of the books of other writers that are based on Lovecraft's mythos.

It is my own conviction that Lovecraft was more than merely a writer of horror stories. I have come to believe that he was a sleeping seer who drew forth from his dreams archetypal realities that lie on the edges of human consciousness, and which have found expression in various veiled forms in our religious myths. Magic deals with such archetypes and the potencies they embody. Through magic they can be summoned and even manipulated for human purposes. Such was the greatest secret wisdom of the priests of ancient Egypt, who not only worshipped their gods, but actively directed their power. The same may be done with the Old Ones, for the considerable benefit of those willing to invoke them.

The Old Ones may care nothing for the hopes and fears of the human race, but magic cares nothing about the Old Ones and their purposes. It simply works. This has always been its ultimate justification, and is the reason it has survived unchanged in its essential methods from the beginning of human history down to the present day. Even Nyarlathotep is not immune to its influence, since it calls upon the very laws that underlie reality itself. These are not the physical laws described by Newton, but are much older laws that have never been articulated, but are intuitively understood by the human mind.

A measure of the reality of Lovecraft's creations, the *Necronomicon* and the Old Ones, is their continuing celebrity. With each year that passes, they receive ever greater attention from the general public. Their acceptance into the body of Western esoteric practice was inevitable, and has been going on for decades. The magic of the Old Ones is still evolving, and is consequently in a state of flux. Eventually it will become more stable, and will attain the status of a recognized branch of Western magic. However, at present it is still viewed with skepticism and disapproval by many serious practitioners. In some small way I hope this grimoire will help to legitimize the chaos magic of the Old Ones, which in my view represents a natural, and indeed an inevitable, evolution in the course of Western occultism.

Book of the North Gate:
Knowledge

The Old Ones

The Old Ones were, the Old Ones are, and the Old Ones shall be. Great is their favor toward those who serve them, but greater still their malice against their foes. They walk the earth when the walls between worlds weaken and the gates of Yog-Sothoth swing wide. At twilight they walk, and in the mists of morning before the ascent of the sun. When moon and sun cross paths on the dragon's head and again on the dragon's tail, they walk. Upon the equinoxes they walk while the seasons of the year hang in balance. Corn is pressed down in the fields where they pass, and trees torn up by their roots. The ground shakes with the rumble of distant thunder, and the air is sharp with the stench of burning brimstone.

By this odor may you know them when they pass near, for no eye can see their unnatural flesh without the aid of sorcery. They are not of this world but of higher worlds, and extend themselves downward into our space the way a man reaches into the depths of a pool. No fish swimming beneath the surface can know when or where the hand will enter the water, or the place it goes when it is withdrawn, nor does the shape of the hand reveal the greater form of the creature to which it is joined. By their tracks on the sands also shall you know them. Legs thick as the trunks of mighty oaks bear up bodies vaster than the largest beast, yet end in five small pads that press into the ground the pattern of a pentalpha.

The Old Ones possess the power of flight, not by means of wings, for wings they have none, but by lifting their great bodies upward into the air with the force of their thoughts alone. They are blind in normal vision, and aeons before the rise of the race of man they dwelt in great cities behind stone walls that lacked windows. Yet they possess senses unnatural to this world that inform them of their surroundings. Few sages have glimpsed them by alchemy or art magic, but those few who dare to write on this forbidden matter declare their bodies to be an ovoid mass of writhing tendrils.

Long ago the Old Ones made war against a time-spanning race from a world called Yith. Great is the power of the Old Ones but greater still was the science of Yith, for all knowledge both past and future lay open to them. The Yithians banished to exile beneath the ground all those Old Ones who had dwelt on the surface of this world in windowless stone cities, sealing the entrances to their caverns with massive doors of black stone. There were other Old Ones not of the cities who took no part in the war, but fled into the heavens through the gates of Yog-Sothoth. The Yithians made no attempt to pursue them. In this way the Old Ones were divided. Those bound to this world by the craft of the Yithians endure below, deep under the ruins of the bygone cities of the time lords, but the Old Ones who did not take part in the war continue to dwell in the airy heights between this world and the higher worlds. Only now and then, when the walls between worlds thin and the gates gape, do they descend to walk in wild places as of old, unseen and unknown.

They cannot long tolerate the surface of this world, for with the passage of aeons the stars have gone wrong in the sky and send down rays poisonous to the alien flesh of the Old Ones. Their old foes, the Yithians, have departed into the future, but the Old Ones are unable to claim their heritage until the stars complete their helical turnings and once more come right in the heavens, as they were of old. Then will the gates of Yog-Sothoth open wide, and the Old Ones descend from the sky and ascend from their crypts to rebuild their windowless cities upon the ruins that remain, and rule this world and all that subsist upon it. Men shall become their slaves, as they were when mighty Cthulhu cast his thoughts across land and sea into their dreams, before R'lyeh sank beneath the waves.

Long have the Old Ones who dwell in the heights sought to breed in the wombs of mortal women hybrids that can tolerate the poison of the stars. To those who aid them in this purpose they grant occult knowledge and power over other men. Sometimes these hybrid offspring resemble their fathers, and walk the earth vast and invisible, while others favor their mothers and wear shapes that approximate the human body. They lack purpose until inhabited by the minds of the dwellers in the heights, and then they seek to fulfill the great labor of the Old Ones, the Work of the Trapezohedron, the reason for which that race traveled across the vasts of space and through many dimensions of reality to reside on this globe. The children of men who aid them in their work are rewarded. Those who hinder them are punished.

By the Long Chant of the *Necronomicon* is the gate of Yog-Sothoth opened, and the way laid bare for the Old Ones to descend into their prepared vessels of lower flesh, both those of mixed blood and those wholly human. Only mortals who have prepared themselves are worthy to carry for a time the spirits of the Old Ones and serve their great work of restoration, the elevation of the fallen queen of heaven to her empty throne. No mortal possessed by an Old One can bear the presence of that spirit for more than a cycle of the moon without madness. They are ancient beyond reckoning and their alien thoughts are not wholesome to the minds of men, but rot the tissues of the brain and render them down to a putrid slime.

Great in the heavens are the Old Ones, low in the dust is man, but higher than mankind are those men who dedicate themselves in service to the great work of the Old Ones, the cleansing of this world that will alone restore her purity, and allow her elevation back to her former high estate, from which she fell into this pit, where she is ceaselessly defiled by life.

The Fallen Earth

Before the glistening effluvium of this universe spilled forth from the cosmic egg, the globe upon which we dwell was the goddess Barbelzoa, beloved and only daughter of he whose true name may not be spoken, but who is called in the tongue of the Old Ones, as it is used among our race, Azathoth. She sat upon the left hand of the throne of creation, and her beauty and wisdom were the twin shining stars of her eyes, so resplendent that no shadow could endure to approach to the throne. The music of her father's flute trilled forth with pure harmonies, and the twelve gigantic gods who dance upon empty space about the throne, sustaining the web of realities with their measured steps, continued with grace and decorum. The trilling notes of the flute spiraled outward unsullied and brought forth a universe filled with bright stars.

The chief messenger and soul of the dancing gods, who is named Nyarlathotep in the tongue of the Old Ones as it is used by men, looked upon Barbelzoa from his throne seat at the right hand of Azathoth, and he desired to possess her purity. Behind the back of her father, he took the virgin goddess by force, in a way that is not like the way of men, but is without the joining of flesh. He gained nothing by his treachery, for her brightness died within his darkness and left behind it only a bitterness on his tongue. In her shame, the goddess could not bear to face wise Azathoth on his throne, who could see into all hearts. She cast herself despairing down from the mount of the triple wisdom seat, down the ninety-three steps and over the edge of the abyss into the wilderness of stars.

The lower she fell, the more of her shining substance turned to dull and solid matter. Nyarlathotep pursued her like a stooping dragon. She heard his cry of rage in her mind and pressed her transformed body of dense matter around herself to conceal her shining nature. Tighter and tighter she wrapped her solidifying form around herself, so that she became a globe no different in outward features from millions of other globes that revolve around the stars spun forth on the music of her father's flute. The weight of matter pressing upon her soul sent her into a deep sleep that is like death. This she did not anticipate, but she could not escape it. In this sleep she dreams, and watches in her dreams what transpires upon the surface of the sphere that is her material body, but she never remembers her true name, or how she cast herself from a high estate down through the gateways of many dimensions into this hellish plane.

When Azathoth learned of Barbelzoa's plunge into the depths of matter, his grief drove him mad. With his own fingernails he raked out his eyes, and in sympathy the twelve dancing gods became blind. His flute shrieked and cracked, so that it no longer gave forth pure notes, but forever after made music that was imperfect. He tore off his fine robes and squatted naked and disheveled on his throne, which turned black from the blackness of his despair. He forgot himself in madness. His hair became matted, his body clotted with his own filth. He could not cease to play his flute, for that is his very reason to exist, but the music that came forth was disordered, and caused the dancing of the twelve blind gods to stumble and falter. The creations that arose from their dance were flawed.

After measureless ages of searching the length and breadth of the cosmos, Nyarlathotep found the sphere of Barbelzoa circling a small but ancient yellow star, far removed from the center of creation. In spite of all his arts, he failed to awaken her from her dreaming slumber at the center of this world. He called upon the servants of his kind who are known as the Old Ones to raise this sphere from the pit of matter to the high seat from which she had fallen, but the Old Ones were frustrated by the countless forms of life that had arisen to inhabit the lands and seas of its surface. So much corporeal life could not be lifted through the highest gate.

Nyarlathotep then commanded that the surface of the earth be wiped clean of all life, but before the Old Ones could fulfill his command, they were attacked by the time-travelers from Yith, who are wisest of all races in the universe and potent in warfare. The Old Ones were defeated and their forces split, some imprisoned in caverns beneath the ground and others sheltering themselves between the spheres of the heavens behind the sealed gates of Yog-Sothoth. Before they could reunite their forces, the stars went wrong in the heavens, and the colors of their conjoined rays became poisonous to the alien flesh of the Old Ones. The Yithians departed into the distant future, but the Old Ones remain, trapped by the stars and by time itself.

The great work of the Old Ones is to sterilize this world of all life, purifying it so that it is made fit to elevate through the highest gate of Yog-Sothoth. Matter may with some awkwardness pass through the lower gates, but so much matter cannot be elevated through the final gate to the throne of creation. Only living matter that has become mingled with the substance of the Old Ones, and in this way transformed into hybrids half of humanity and half of the Old Ones, becomes fit for this transition. This intermingling may be accomplished not merely through the mingling of flesh, but through the mind and soul, which have the power to purify the body.

Nyarlathotep rages. He holds the mad Azathoth in contempt, but cannot kill him and take his place on the highest seat of the black throne of chaos, for if the flute of Azathoth ceased to trill its notes, and the twelve blind gods halted their dance, everything would come to an end in darkness and silence, even Nyarlathotep himself. He cannot possess the goddess Barbelzoa, for she is protected by her armor of dense matter, formed from her own solidified body, which has become her prison, and perhaps her tomb. Nyarlathotep strides across the sands of this world in the shape of a man, and he rages and schemes how to raise this globe with its shining core up to the place from which it fell so that the goddess shall be released.

First, he must restore the rule of the Old Ones upon the earth. This he seeks to accomplish through the use of human agents, and other agents who dwell in the deep places of the world that are not human. Yog-Sothoth aids him in his work, but not always willingly, for Yog-Sothoth did not approve of the violation of the goddess. Yog-Sothoth loves order and harmony and laments its loss. He aids Nyarlathotep in the hope that harmony will be restored to the cosmos when Barbelzoa awakens, but he is no friend to Nyarlathotep, and will act to frustrate the messenger of the dancing gods when opportunity presents itself.

Men and women who are wise serve Nyarlathotep, for his service is the royal road to wealth and power, and to forbidden knowledge of the lost arts of magic. Yet they never fail to give honor to Yog-Sothoth who is the gate through which all travelers must pass. Even more do they honor mad Azathoth, who is the source of all power, including that of Nyarlathotep and Yog-Sothoth. Remember this and be wise: Yog-Sothoth opens the gate, Nyarlathotep shows the way, but Azathoth on his black throne, at the center of the chaos his madness has created, is the fulfillment of the quest. When the fallen Barbelzoa awakens and is restored to the left hand of her father, his madness will end, and true service will be remembered.

Azathoth

Azathoth is the leader of the twelve dancing gods, the greatest of these archons and the creator of our universe, which is formed on the nothingness of space itself from intervals of sound and silence. Before the fall of his daughter Barbelzoa, who in her self-chosen exile became this earthly sphere, he piped forth the fabric of creation with elegant and stately harmonies that became beautiful things, but his grief at the loss of his daughter drove him mad, and in his drooling idiocy his music is shrill with discordances, and becomes things that are imperfect. The left-hand seat of the triple throne remains vacant. The gods continue to dance, but their steps falter and hesitate.

The blind idiot god on his black throne is still the source of all that occurs. Nothing can be done without his approval, but in his madness he gives it capriciously. Nyarlathotep on the right-hand seat of the triple throne rages at his own impotence, for no matter how vast his ambition and his lust for power, he is dependent on the approval of Azathoth, and without it he remains impotent. By lies and tricks and beguilements he wins the favor of the idiot god, who pipes the dark purposes of Nyarlathotep into being without considering the consequences of his plots.

Witches and wizards carried through the gates of Yog-Sothoth in dreams to the foot of the black throne by Nyarlathotep claim that Azathoth has the shape of a corpulent man deformed and stunted like a dwarf, but many times the size of the tallest giant that dwells in our sphere. His face is compressed and misshapen, his blind eyes are pits that ooze mucus, his blubbery lips drool as he pipes his cracked flute of bone. Rolls of fat hang down his filthy chest, and his matted black hair dangles across his rounded shoulders. His skin is gray, for he has long dwelled in darkness. The twelve who dance around the throne upon the air issue forth sighing breaths of sorrow as they pass, lamenting for the old times of beauty and light.

All these forms are no more than appearances glimpsed in dreams, for no man has stood before the throne in his own flesh and lived to tell of it. Nyarlathotep carries up the souls of those who swear to do him service, so that their names can be confirmed in the great book that is kept beneath the black throne, the book that is called the *Necronomicon*. Their bodies he does not carry up, for the fiery heat of the center of all creation and destruction would strip the flesh from their bones and leave them no more than ashes ground under the feet of the dancing gods.

There is a secret teaching that declares Azathoth to be the very vortex at the center of chaos from which all emerged, and into which all returns. His music is said to be no more than the eternal howling of this maelstrom, and that all who venture near it are drawn in and consumed as though by a hungry mouth, without discrimination as to rank or kind. The universe itself is said to be no more than excrement cast forth from the anus of the naked idiot god, which in the fullness of time he will consume in his madness, and thus repeat the cycle of creation and destruction.

The true name of Azathoth is known to but a few, and is not to be spoken aloud, for to speak his true name is to invoke his confirmation of whatever is willed, either for good or ill. His true name is the pattern of all creation. In his madness he gives his fiat capriciously, so that those who invoke his approval oftentimes wish they had remained silent. Even Nyarlathotep invokes the name of Azathoth with dread, never knowing if it will enable his purposes or frustrate them, and always gnashing his teeth at the necessity to seek the force of realization for his judgments from the idiot god. For it is only the music of Azathoth that makes or destroys. His madness renders Azathoth unpredictable, and causes all magics to be uncertain in their efficacy.

The true name of Azathoth is called the tetractys among Greek philosophers, but is known as the Tetragrammaton (in the Greek tongue) among the Hebrews. It is represented by ten dots in four rows, arranged in the form of a triangle with a single dot in the top row, two in the row beneath, three in the third row, and four in the final row, so that they define a triangle with equal sides. However, the tetractys is only half of the mystery of the name. The full mystery is revealed when a second tetractys is inverted and laid over the first, so that a figure is defined by the resulting thirteen dots that has the shape of a star with six points.

The top row has one dot, but the second either two or four, depending on which of the interlocking triangles is favored, the third row three dots, the fourth row either

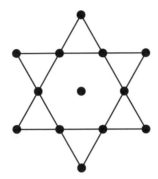

True Name of Azathoth

two or four, depending on which triangle is brought foremost in the mind, and the final fifth row has a single dot. This figure is the same when viewed from the top or from the bottom. The first and fifth rows are identical, composed of the monad, which are both the source and the final termination. The second and fourth rows are also the same, but they are dual in their natures, either twofold or fourfold. The third row is shared by both the upright and the inverted tetractys.

This geometric figure may be turned so that any of its six points is uppermost, and it will have the same structure. These six points represent the six directions of space, which form pairs of opposites that are north-south, east-west, up-down. The inner circle of six dots about the central dot represent the seven lords of the Old Ones, with Azathoth at the center of all; the inner and outer circles of twelve dots stand for the twelve blind gods that dance about the throne of Azathoth. The Hebrews have written of this in their Kabbalah, but obscurely to conceal it from the foolish. This star of thirteen points is the true name of Azathoth, which has an articulation of sounds that can destroy the universe when rightly voiced.

This is the seal of Azathoth, by which he is to be adored and petitioned. It differs from his sigil, which is also based upon the letters of his common name but is

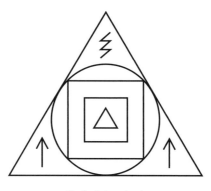

Seal of Azathoth

extracted from the magic square of the sun. This seal is built up from the primal letter glyphs in his common name and is the soul of that name. Use it in all works and rituals done in his name and by his authority.

Azathoth is best invoked for works that fall under the authority of the sphere of the sun, such as works of integration and wholeness, of self-expression and self-

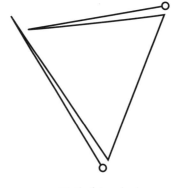

Sigil of Azathoth

awareness. The place in space naturally ruled by him is the center, which lies at the heart of the six directions.

Nyarlathotep

He who is the messenger and the soul of the blind archons who dance about the black throne of Azathoth is drawn to this earth because it is the fallen body of the goddess Barbelzoa, who cast herself from heaven into the starry pit of matter. He schemes and plots how to wipe our world clean of all material life, so that it may be elevated back to its original high estate, but he is powerless to act except at the capricious whims of mad Azathoth. He whispers his purposes into the ear of Azathoth, but some the blind idiot god heeds, and to others he remains deaf.

Even so, Nyarlathotep is the most potent of all the Old Ones. Before the fall, it had been his custom to sit on the right-hand side of the throne of Azathoth and execute the will of Azathoth on the cosmos. Now, Azathoth has no conscious will of his own, and Nyarlathotep follows his own purposes. He likes to walk up and down upon the earth in the form of a man, which he appropriated ages ago in ancient Egypt. The original soul of the pharaoh was consumed in his cold fire, and Nyarlathotep took up habitation in his shell of flesh, which he rendered deathless by means of his alchemy.

It is within the power of Nyarlathotep to take on whatever shape or form he desires, and to move through the gateways of Yog-Sothoth freely. No world or dimension of reality is forbidden to him, yet no matter how wide his wanderings, he is drawn back always to this world in memory of the goddess who sleeps at its heart. When Azathoth pipes his music, and the blind gods dance, Nyarlathotep must fulfill their purposes, for he is their messenger. He rebels against this servitude and seeks to bring about purposes of his own, for his advantage or amusement. Sometimes he succeeds, but sometimes he fails, for Azathoth is capricious in his madness. What man or god may know the song he will choose to play?

Nyarlathotep is given power as messenger of the blind gods of creation over the gods of earth that have arisen from the desires and aspirations of mankind. The gods of earth are bound to the earth. They are formed from the dreams of Barbelzoa. She hears in her sleep the crying out of humanity for justice and truth and her dreaming mind brings forth gods and goddesses that are composed of these principles. She hears the groans of lust and the cries of war, and her dreaming mind shapes gods and goddesses of love or hate. All gods of earth are mere fancies of dreaming Barbelzoa, shadows of her sleepy thoughts. They arose in response to the yearnings of humanity, and to humanity and its needs they remain forever bound.

Nyarlathotep resents these earthly deities and has gathered them together in a great throne room in the place known as Kadath in the Cold Waste. He keeps them as pets for his own amusement, and it is only with his approval that they are permitted to answer the prayers of mankind. In this way he seeks to make himself into a smaller image of Azathoth, for as Azathoth rules the cosmos and all its dimensions, so Nyarlathotep seeks to rule this world, which is the body of the dreaming goddess. He hates the gods of earth, for in them is a nobility and purity that he lacks within himself. They are powerless to resist him, and tremble at the sound of his footsteps.

Of all the playthings Nyarlathotep has found upon this world, none amuses him more than the race of man. He is known among men as the Crawling Chaos, because his appearance is often followed by madness. Those who walk in deserts or through wildernesses by night sometimes meet this god and converse with him, never knowing with whom they spoke, or how near they were to death. It is the caprice of Nyarlathotep to hold conversations with men or women when the mood strikes his fancy, and then he may impart to them arcane secrets of precious value. Yet if they approach him when he is angry, he will reach out his bony black hand and touch them upon the forehead, and their bodies will at once crumble to flakes of black dust as their souls are eaten by him.

The god may be recognized by his black robes that are wrapped about his long and thin body. Often he walks the desert veiled, but those who have glimpsed behind the veil run mad and scream that he has no face. Yet he may put on any face he chooses as a mask, for none of them are his own. His true face was once carved upon the head of the great statue of Egypt known as the Sphinx, before the pharaoh Kephren in a fit of fury commanded that it be struck off, and placed his own image on the head of the statue. It is whispered that the Order of the Sphinx preserves his true image in their subterranean vaults. Who can say, for those who venture beneath its tail never emerge.

Seal of Nyarlathotep

This is the seal of Nyarlathotep that is to be inscribed on all instruments and charms devoted to his service or worship. It is not to be confused with his sigil that is extracted from his name upon the magic square of Mercury. Both have power to attract the notice of the god, though neither will guarantee his wayward favor, which he sometimes extends to those who worship him or serve him, but sometimes with-holds. Only the Great Seal of the Old Ones can compel him to obedience. Think long before you use it. Nyarlathotep never forgets an insult, and never forgives. It is better to propitiate him with offerings and sacrifices and prayers of praise. Those he chooses to favor wax great in wealth and authority, for a time. Eventually the interest of the Creeping Chaos wanders, and he withdraws his favor and seeks other amuse-ments, leaving them to their own fate.

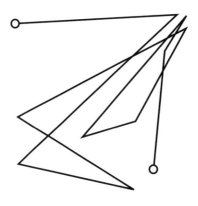

Sigil of Nyarlathotep

It is best to petition Nyarlathotep in matters that fall under the authority of the sphere of Mercury, for there is harmony between the affairs of this sphere and the nature of Nyarlathotep, who is a messenger for the dancing archons. The magic square of Mercury has power to attract his notice, as does his sigil formed on that square from his name. Nyarlathotep does not dwell in the sphere of Mercury—the length and breadth of the entire cosmos is his home—but he has a harmony with this sphere that may be used by practitioners of magic in their dealings with him. Of the six directions, that most in accord with this god is the depths, and this is as it should be, for he is called the Creeping Chaos.

Yog-Sothoth

The remaining of the three high lords of the archons is Yog-Sothoth, god of portals. He rules all goings in, and all comings out. Doors are the mouth of Yog-Sothoth, and windows are his eyes. Whenever a threshold is crossed, this god is aware, and it can only be crossed when he permits it. He is both the gate and the key. None may pass through a portal that he has locked. He rules transitions between spheres and between worlds, and regulates them as he sees fit, according to his own sense of necessity that is conditioned by the changing patterns of the heavens.

On certain festival dates the gates of Yog-Sothoth swing wide, but on other dates they remain shut. Chief among the openings is the festival known as May Eve, occurring on the final night of the month of April, and almost as potent for openings is the festival known as the Eve of All Hallows, occurring on the final night of the month of October. In addition to these mighty festivals, upon the spring and autumnal equinoxes the separation between worlds becomes thin and easily crossed. At these dates in the wheel of the year, the gates of Yog-Sothoth may be opened by rites of worship, by sacrifices, and by the use of the Long Chant that is written in some lesser-known copies of the *Necronomicon*—for all earthly editions of this black book beneath the throne of Azathoth are imperfect copies, and all are incomplete.

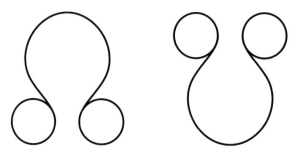

Head and Tail of the Dragon

The symbol called the Head of the Dragon is potent in opening the gates of Yog-Sothoth, whatever kind they may be, but the symbol known as the Tail of the Dragon closes the gates and seals them shut against the transition of those things best kept on the other side. When a gate is opened, creatures who wait for just this chance attempt to force their way through. If they are quick, they may succeed. Be ever watchful for their lurkings and their advances. Do not be deceived by their blandishments and lies, for they use whatever trick offers itself if it will aid in their transitions. When a gate is passed, it is best to seal it shut by forming the Tail of the Dragon with a gesture of the right hand upon the air. Yog-Sothoth is vigilant against the greater outrages, but he may fail to notice the lesser outrages.

Yog-Sothoth remains invisible except when he opens a gateway, and then he appears as a gathering of rotating iridescent spheres that intersect and overlap, their periods and proportions defining the conditions under which the gate was opened, and the place to which it leads, for those able to read them. Their harmonies are mathematical and musical. The opening of a gateway is not in the sounds of these turning spheres, nor in the silences between the sounds, but in the ever-shifting balance created between the sounds and the silences. Each circle is a world. Where they touch and overlap are gates. Such is the face of Yog-Sothoth, which is the face of the cosmos.

When the soul of a man is liberated from his house of flesh and bone, which happens during dreams and at those times when through some accident the soul is struck out by violent force and flies free, Nyarlathotep may lead the soul to any place or any world, even to the throne of chaos itself, but the Creeping Chaos is only able to act as guide with the sufferance of Yog-Sothoth, who may seal the gates against him if he so chooses. Yog-Sothoth cannot be bullied, not even by Nyarlathotep, and he can only be petitioned by rites and sacrifices on those dates and times that are conducive to the opening of the gates. When the stars conspire in their windings to deny transition, Yog-Sothoth must obey. Not even the Long Chant will move him at these unfavorable times.

Seal of Yog-Sothoth

Use the seal of Yog-Sothoth to summon the god of portals. He is best called within a stone circle upon a high place, for he dwells in the upper firmament, and descends through the spheres to approach the earth. His greatest harmony is with the sphere of the sun. He is therefore best petitioned by rites and sacrifices in matters that pertain to this sphere, and in all matters that require transition from one place or condition to another. The magic square of the sun has power in his rites. The direction of space that has greatest affinity for his nature is the heights, for he dwells in the upper regions.

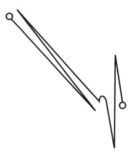

Sigil of Yog-Sothoth

Remember, Nyarlathotep is the guide, but Yog-Sothoth is the gate. Physical travel between worlds is rare and fraught with danger. It is better to use the gates of this god to travel in the spirit, in a body of astral light. This can be done in dreams, or by the deliberate projection of the astral shell. Call upon Yog-Sothoth to open the gate, but on Nyarlathotep to lead the way. Those who pass through the gates in their physical shells seldom return, and if they do come back after the long passage of years, they often run mad.

Yig

Among the lesser lords of the Old Ones who do not dwell near the throne of chaos but upon or near this fallen world that shields the dreaming goddess, Yig is the most distant and difficult to understand. Some sages deny that he is even one of the Old Ones, but if he is not of their pure blood, it is certain that he is of their fraternity, for Yig and the Old Ones have had dealings since the beginning of time. In the vast subterranean land of K'n-yan, Yig is worshipped alongside Cthulhu with equal reverence by the alien race that dwells there.

Yig is father to all serpents, and those of serpent kind such as the salamanders and the dragons that dwell between the worlds and are glimpsed by men but seldom. He can walk the earth unseen, but when he puts on form, it is that of a great serpent, or sometimes that of a man with the head of a snake. All lesser serpents bend to his will and do his bidding. He seldom speaks but prefers to hiss in the voice of his many children. When he enters the body of a man and drives out his soul, the possessed man falls to the ground and writhes his limbs sinuously, making hissing sounds with his lips and flicking out his tongue to taste the air.

It is within the power of Yig to breed with mortal women and engender hybrids in their wombs. This he does seldom, since there is little value in such servants who bear a form mostly human but lack intelligence and are mute. They writhe all their long lives on their naked bellies, and prefer to lie curled up in dark places, where they sleep and perchance dream the dreams of serpents. Their blood has virtue in prolonging the normal span of life, and it is for this reason alone that they are sought. Those who displease Yig by mocking him, or by mistreating or slaying his sinuous children, are killed by the bites of many serpents, or sometimes are driven mad by the visitation of the god himself.

Yig knows the ancient secrets that lie hidden in cold and dark places at the edges of the world. He knows the ways that lead deep through the twisting bowels of the earth, and what forgotten things still dwell there. His memory is long, and he never forgets. He is the most ancient of the lesser lords, almost as old as Nyarlathotep himself. He favors those who do him worship, and enjoys the dancing and songs of his worshippers. Rhythmic drumming is the music best liked by Yig, and rhythmic chants are his preferred song. Those who adore him also adore his children and refrain from doing them harm, for every serpent, even the smallest and meekest, is mighty Yig himself in a form of flesh. Their eyes are his eyes, their teeth are his teeth.

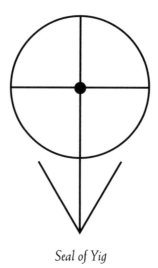

Seal of Yig

Use the seal of Yig to summon and propitiate the god with praise and pledges of service. He never sleeps, for his eyes never close, and he is always watchful. When called with proper rites and offerings, he will come. It is easy to win his friendship, but woe to him who chances to step upon a snake, for it is certain that Yig will punish him.

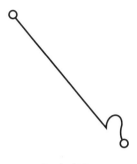

Sigil of Yig

The harmony of Yig is the sphere of Saturn, which is the most remote of the spheres of the heavens recognized in the ancient texts. Call upon this god in works that pertain to this distant sphere, such as matters of arcane wisdom, prudence, renewal, and long life. The magic square of Saturn is useful in his rites. It does not possess power over the god, but it resonates with the nature of the god and acts as a beacon inviting his approach. The direction of space most naturally in harmony with Yig is the gateway of the north.

Shub-Niggurath

Alone among the greater and lesser lords of the Old Ones, Shub-Niggurath is female. She is the mother of monsters. The other lords of the Old Ones, and many other gods besides, such as the toad-god Tsathoggua, breed offspring in her womb, for she will lie with anyone who offers. Her common title is the Goat With A Thousand Young. Like the goat, she is ever ready to copulate. Azathoth, lord of the black throne whose true name must not be spoken, is her spouse, and they remain linked in perpetual sexual congress on a higher plane, so that the womb of Shub-Niggurath is never empty, but forever spills forth its chaotic fruits. Yet she is an adulteress and under the veil of Azathoth's madness she lusts and is sated with myriads of strange gods.

In dreams she comes to those who seethe with unsatisfied desire. To men she comes as a beautiful woman in the beginning of the communion, but as she grows more certain of her power over her enthralled lovers, she lets her mask slip and reveals her bestial countenance. By then her lovers are too deeply mired in excesses of the senses to reject her odious embrace. The men of her cult even come to prefer her inhuman form. To women she appears as a demon of lust to seduce them, but if they resist she violates them in their dreams. Shub-Niggurath has the organs of both sexes at her loins, so that she can lie with both male and female.

Among the witches of Europe who practiced black magic in past centuries, she was known as the Black Goat of the Woods. Priests in their ignorance called her the Devil, but those of the black covens, where rituals of chaotic magic were worked in circles of blood using the fat of murdered infants, worshipped her as their dark goddess of the black moon. The waning crescent is her sign, the scent of monkshood and nightshade her perfume, the goat her favored creature. She presides over the black witch cults with Nyarlathotep, who amuses himself with the worship of men and with instructing them in the doing of chaotic works. He was known long ago as the Black Man from his custom of wearing a black robe and cloak, and veiling his face from view with a black mask. When a candidate witch is brought before Nyarlathotep for marking, he takes that person, who lies entranced while the soul leaves his body, through the gates of Yog-Sothoth to the black throne at the center of chaos, and there the candidate inscribes his name in the *Necronomicon* in blood. For this reason the *Necronomicon* has been called "the book of dead names," since all who sign it relinquish the petty intents of their present lives to serve a higher purpose, and become as the walking dead who dwell not in this life but in the next. A more precise translation of the title would be "the book of the laws of the dead," for by its power those who sign it are bound for eternity, and must remain obedient to the laws written on its pages.

Shub-Niggurath takes many forms in dreams, some beautiful and others horrifying. She possesses no true form, but all her shapes and attributes merely signify aspects of her nature. As her spouse, Azathoth, is at his primal essence the very vortex of chaos itself, so Shub-Niggurath is the womb of creation, which has become corrupted since the fall of Barbelzoa and the madness of Azathoth. Before the violation and descent in sinfulness of the goddess Barbelzoa, the womb of Shub-Niggurath gave forth noble and true offspring. Barbelzoa was her first-born. The madness of Azathoth made her womb murky with swirling chaos and intoxicated her with lust, so that she breeds with anything, and her womb generates in kind.

Necromancers who have pierced with keen sight beneath the layers of her many masks say that she has the horned, hairy head of a goat, coupled with a goat's hairy legs and cloven hooves, but the soft arms and rounded breasts of a beautiful woman. At her groin the two sexes strangely merge. Some have thought to link her with the Baphomet of the Knights Templar, but that is a mystery not to be revealed. By her odor you may know that she is present even when she stands invisible. She has the harsh scent of rut, like to the musk of the deer. Her sexual parts forever drip with lust, even though her belly is perpetually domed with the life growing in her womb, nor is her womb ever empty, but as soon as it gives forth its fruit becomes again impregnated.

Seal of Shub-Niggurath

The seal of Shub-Niggurath is formed from the primal shapes of the letters in her name, and has power to summon her awareness and to petition her for favors in her natural sphere of desire and pleasure. The planet most in accord with her nature is Venus, and for this reason the magic square of Venus, with the sigil of Shub-Niggurath that may be generated from her name upon that square, has power in her rituals and charms. The direction of the six directions of space that is most in harmony with her nature and purposes is that of the east, the quarter of spring, the lush green seedlings of which express her endless fertility.

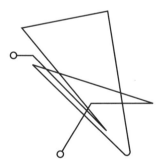

Sigil of Shub-Niggurath

Worship of Shub-Niggurath gives potency in lovemaking, attraction of lovers, the power of fascination and glamour of appearances, and intense and varied pleasures of kinds unknown to other mortals. She may be called upon in matters of attraction, affection, desire, sensation, and pleasure. Those who worship her must beware the wiles of the Black Man, who will try to steal away their loyalty to this goddess, and then betray them with tricks, for Nyarlathotep is ever the trickster, and to sow confusion among mankind is his delight.

Cthulhu

Cthulhu flew on his vast leathern wings across the gulf of space to conquer and rule this world. He had no other purpose. He revels in combat, warfare, bloodshed, and death. Conquest is his way, and the way of his spawn, who are like him in their general appearance, but smaller. Whereas Cthulhu is as large as a mountain, his spawn are little bigger than horses or cows. They also possess wings for flying through the air, and through the dark emptiness of space. They are said to resemble the octopus, but this is true only of their heads, which are hung in the front of their faces with tentacles that lift and writhe about in the air, for they are all by nature dwellers on the surface of the earth and in the air. It is only misadventure that cast them below the waves of the sea, which they loathe and despise with a passionate hatred, for this water prevents them from sending forth their thoughts across the face of the world to control those who worship them.

When Cthulhu descended from between the stars to the dreaming earth, he found it ruled by the Elder Things, an ancient race possessing deep wisdom that also came to this world from the stars, but long before the coming of Cthulhu and his spawned army. Cthulhu thought to easily destroy the Elder Things, but to his amazement and dismay he found their arts of warfare equal to his own. His spawn swept against their slaves that are called shoggoths the way an ocean wave sweeps toward the rocks of the shore, and it broke upon them just as a wave breaks and falls back in frustration. The shoggoth is the strongest creature that has ever lived, and deathless. Not even the spawn could prevail against them.

To end the war more quickly, the Elder Things were gracious and ceded to Cthulhu and his spawn the newly risen lands of the Pacific Ocean that formed chains of islands. With these the war god was content to bide his time, for he never ceased to plot the overthrow of the Elder Things and the conquest of this entire world. He and his spawn, which are smaller buddings of himself from his own body, sent forth their thoughts into the dreams of the other thinking creatures of the earth, bringing them into subjugation and servitude, until all worshipped Cthulhu as a god, including the hairy ape-like beings that would later become men.

Alas for Cthulhu, the stars changed their pattern in the heavens, and sent down poisonous rays to vex him. He used his magic to place his spawn and himself into a sleep that was like death, but in his dreams he continued to send forth his thoughts and to rule his worshippers. A second disaster struck, one unforeseen in spite of all his wisdom and ancient experience. The island of R'lyeh sank beneath the waves to the bottom of the sea with Cthulhu and all his spawn locked within their stone houses, dreaming their strange dreams. The mass of water held back his thoughts and the thoughts of the spawn. There was no way to call his worshippers to release him should the stars came right once again in the heavens. So Cthulhu and his spawn continue to lie on sunken R'lyeh, deep beneath the waves, almost forgotten by men, but dreaming still of warfare and conquest.

Statues of Cthulhu, carved from green stone that is not native to this world, reveal the strange shape of the dreaming god. He has a massive, bulging head that is soft and pulsing on the top, with six small eyes on the front, and below them a tangle of slender writhing tentacles resembling a nest of serpents that conceals his mouth. From his back hang his enormous wings, like those of a bat that are folded close. His body is like the body of a man corpulent and of solid frame, but his hands and feet end in claws that are longer than the tusks of the greatest elephant. His flesh is said by those who claim to have glimpsed it in dreams to be like cloudy green glass that lets light pass through, and similar to jelly beneath the touch. But when it is cut it heals itself almost instantly and reforms. No injury of a normal kind can harm Cthulhu or his spawn. They are deathless, since they do not live as we know life.

Those men who worship him have formed a cult in the far corners of the world, and pass down the ancient knowledge of R'lyeh. They worship his statues, but their priests receive no instruction from him, except at rare times when the gate of Yog-Sothoth opens upon R'lyeh, and they travel to the sunken citadel of their mighty lord and hold communication with him in their dreaming minds. Then does Cthulhu instruct them in the rites of his cult. He tells them to wait and watch for the stars to come right in their courses, and for R'lyeh to rise, for these are the signals that the time of slaying is come upon the world again, as it was before the making of man by the Elder Things.

The worship of Cthulhu lends courage and skill in warfare and all forms of battle. In dreams Cthulhu teaches ancient wisdom and ancient magic, for he is the high priest of the Old Ones and well-learned in all their alien arts. Only Nyarlathotep has greater wisdom, but the Crawling Chaos seldom teaches men matters of great value. Cthulhu is generous to his worshippers. He needs them to come and release him and his spawn from their stone houses once R'lyeh rises above the waves. He teaches them the joys of battle and the greater joys of slaying. His cult is fearless and without mercy or kindness. They gladly kill the innocent, and embrace death as a lover.

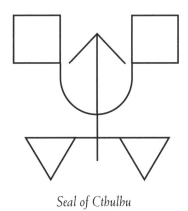

Seal of Cthulhu

Use this seal of the war god to reach him in the depths of your dreams, or when you project your astral form beneath the waves to sunken R'lyeh, where you may hold communication with Cthulhu as he sleeps. The sphere of the heavens most in harmony with his warlike nature is the sphere of Mars. All things martial are suited to form a part of his worship and his rites. Of all the Old Ones, he most delights in sacrifices of blood. It is possible to invoke a shadow of his mind, and in this way take on the fierceness and mercilessness of the warrior god and his spawn. This is useful in achieving victory in battle or in contests. Cthulhu cannot bear to lose any contest. He cannot bear to decline any challenge.

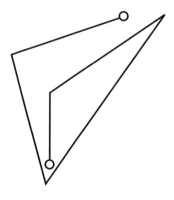

Sigil of Cthulhu

The magic square of the sphere of Mars, and the sigil formed from the name of Cthulhu upon that square are both useful instruments in seeking the aid or teachings of the dreaming god. His natural way among the six directions of space is the south, because its fiery nature accords with his lust for war. A final word of warning. It is possible to invoke a shadow of Cthulhu's mind into your own mind, and in this way take on the force of will, the fearlessness, the aggression, and warlike virtues of the god, but consider well before you attempt this, for Cthulhu glories in slaying and death, and is not fastidious about whom he slays.

Dagon

Dagon dwells in a deep rift below the waters of the Pacific Ocean. Like mighty Cthulhu, he is of vast size with a body as large as the largest of whales, but his nature is unlike that of the war god. Dagon delights in self-command and the attainment of arcane skills, and in the intricate working of metals and the crafting of jewels. He does not make war for sport, but only when it is necessary for the survival of his people. Long ages past, before even Cthulhu and his spawn came to this world, Dagon and his spouse Hydra swam across the sea of space and took up their abode in the deep places of the oceans, where they erected their mighty cities of stone. The Elder Things did not molest them, for they committed no aggression against the crinoid race and their shoggoth slaves.

The womb of Hydra is ever fertile, and brought forth the sons and daughters of Dagon in their teeming myriads. They are like Dagon in shape, and do not resemble Hydra, which no human eye has glimpsed despite the legends that are told in her name. Manlike in body, they have webbed hands and feet, and heads that resemble those of a frog, joined to their shoulders with no neck and having gill slits in their sides. Just as the spawn of Cthulhu resemble their father but are smaller in size, so the children of Dagon resemble him but are in size no larger than men. They are called the Deep Ones, and can live both in the depths of the ocean and in the air on land.

The Deep Ones have long cohabited with human beings and sired hybrid off-spring on their human wives. Men, too, can engender hybrids in the females of Dagon's children. They are in every way human when born, but as they age, they acquire the characteristic sloping brows, wide mouths, and broad noses of those born in unions between humans and Deep Ones. Their skin becomes gray in color and scaled. Gill slits open in the sides of their necks. Eventually they leave the land and go to dwell in the deepest canyons on the ocean floor, where the cities of the Deep Ones are built.

The cults of the Deep Ones among human beings worship both Father Dagon and Mother Hydra. Sacrifices are made to them of young men and women. They swear potent oaths to keep the secret of the Deep Ones forever, and to serve them in all their works. In return the Deep Ones give them gold and the treasures of the oceans, and drive fish into their nets to feed them. This commerce between men and Deep Ones has been carried on for ages. In lost Atlantis, the Deep Ones mated with the noble warrior class of that island kingdom, and gave the people crystal weapons that emitted rays of light to destroy their enemies and enslave them. These weapons were the downfall of Atlantis, for the people grew arrogant and misused them during a civil war that destroyed Atlantis and sent it under the sea. Among the Deep Ones there are those who still live and remember Atlantis, for they are deathless save by accident, poison, or deliberate violence.

The native people of the Pacific Isles ward off the Deep Ones of Dagon with a symbol that they paint or inscribe on flat beach stones. It is abhorrent to the Deep Ones and their great father, and holds power over them. This symbol was created by the Elder Things in case of need, before they knew that Dagon and his children were peaceful and did not seek to make war against the crinoid race. In appearance it is much like the symbol known as the swastika, but with rounded arms instead of arms that are bent at angles.

Charm Against the Deep Ones

No Deep One will cross a threshold that has this symbol upon it. No Deep One will follow a path that has this symbol lying in it. No Deep One will emerge from a beach that is strewn with stones bearing this sacred symbol. It represents the spiral chaotic vortex of Azathoth. Yog-Sothoth recognizes it, and will not open any portal upon which it rests for the passage of the sea dwellers. All transitions are portals to Yog-Sothoth, even transition from the surf to the sand, or progress upon a path. By this sign those islanders who dwell near the cities of the Deep Ones are not molested by them while they are on the land, but when they venture into the waves the Deep Ones exact a vengeance upon them, and for this reason these islanders never swim off the beaches of their islands, or stand in the surf to fish along their reefs.

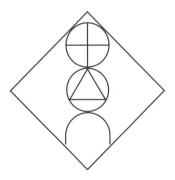

Seal of Dagon

By this seal, formed from the primal shapes of the letters in the sea-god's name, may Dagon be called and petitioned for favors. He is willing to give help to all who ask, but he demands service in return, and sometimes sacrifices. The Deep Ones are not only his children's children, but also his agents on both the seas and the land, who execute his judgments among mortals. Those who wed a Deep One are protected. Those who are born of the union between a human and a Deep One are protected. But those who betray the secrets of this race are pursued and punished.

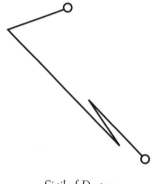

Sigil of Dagon

The sphere of the moon is in greatest accord with the nature of Dagon, which is inclined to dreams and visions, and to artistic accomplishments. The god teaches skills for the curing of sickness and the prolonging of life, and skills for scrying into the future and into hidden matters. Actions that fall under the authority of the moon are suited for the invocation of Dagon and his race. The symbols of the moon lend themselves to use in his rites. Among the six directions of space, the way that is naturally given to Dagon is the west, that quarter of the world associated with the oceans.

The Dancing Gods

The twelve gods who step and twirl and leap about the black throne of chaos in perpetual motion, driven by the rhythms and melodies of Azathoth's flute, are archons to the Old Ones, even as Azathoth himself is the chief archon who created the cosmos. They are of gigantic dimensions and strange disproportions, and their bodies change to reflect the changing moods of their dance. Many are imperfect or deformed since the fall of Barbelzoa and the madness of her grieving father. The anguish of Azathoth is made apparent in their broken shapes. What Azathoth expresses in his music, the dancing gods manifest in their dance.

Their naked bodies shine with iridescent colors. They dance between worlds, so that sometimes their bodies seem a strange sort of translucent flesh, yet at other times they appear a conglutination of colored spheres, similar to the face of Yog-Sothoth that is glimpsed when he opens his gates. Simultaneously they dance in all worlds, all realities, straddling the gates between their thighs. They are blind, as is Azathoth, for they are of the same blood. When he lost his sight and reason, the dancing gods lost their reason and their sight in sympathy, for they are connected to him with ties deeper than his link to the womb of Shub-Niggurath. His music is their food and drink. The notes of his flute are the flesh of their forms, as these trilling notes are all flesh and all stone, everywhere. The cosmos is made of music, and it is the tragedy of creation that the flute of Azathoth is cracked.

The sorcerers and stargazers of the Persians signified the twelve dancing gods in the forms of the zodiac, which they placed in the firmament of fixed stars, above the planets, just as the dancing archons are above the lords of the Old Ones, even above the bowed head of Azathoth himself. Here is a mystery. In the double tetractys that expresses in geometric form the true and secret name of Azathoth, there are thirteen dots. The central dot represents Azathoth on his black throne, and the twelve dots that surround it and form the star of six points stand for the mindless idiot gods who dance, and by their measured steps create and destroy the universe, for there cannot be creation without destruction, or destruction without creation.

Some sages assert that each god simultaneously creates and destroys six universes, and that each universe has five primary planes or dimensions of reality, so that in all the cosmos there are three hundred and sixty dimensions. Others less bound to ancient doctrine assert the planes of being and their gates to be infinite in number. Yog-Sothoth knows the answer, but who shall question the god of portals? It may be that the primary planes that form the structure of creation are of this number, but that the lesser planes are infinite.

These are the names and seals of the twelve dancing gods who rule over the lower hells and the throne of chaos, each commanding his own six universes and their five planes, the subdivision of which is infinite. Before the madness of Azathoth they ruled the pure heavens, but after his fall they rule the lower hells, for he made the heavens into hells, and the higher into the lower. They dance invisible, but sometimes put on forms like masks that express aspects of their natures, and from these masks the zodiac was derived.

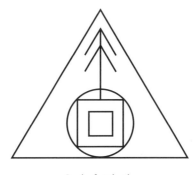

Seal of Athoth

The first is named Athoth, who is surnamed the Reaper for his sharp sickle that he uses to reap souls to torment. He is hairy all over, and wears the horns of the ram on his head. He was placed by the wise Persians in the portion of the zodiac known as Aries, the Ram.

Seal of Harmas

The second is called Harmas, who is surnamed the Eye of the Fire, which glares into the hearts of all who commit acts of evil and chars them to black ash. He has the head of a black cow with a single great red jewel in his forehead, and snarling jaws that drip the foam of madness. His portion of the heavens is that known as Taurus, the Bull.

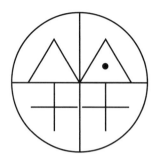

Seal of Galila

The third bears the name Galila, who has the form of a young girl. Upon her left side extends a reddened scar where her conjoined twin brother tore himself away at the closing of the former age of the cosmos. The old wound yet seeps blood, and she sorrows for her loss, even after the passage of countless ages. Her portion is that known as Gemini, the Twins.

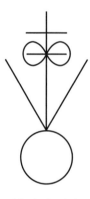

Seal of Yobel

The fourth has the name Yobel. Her shape is monstrous, her skin covered in heavy armored plates of horn, like to the shell of the crab. The Persians have given her the portion of the heavens called Cancer, the Crab.

Seal of Adonaios

The fifth is called Adonaios. He is fierce and red in claw, with a great, angry countenance fringed in golden hair, and a roaring voice that splits the air like thunder. His part of the zodiac is Leo, the Lion.

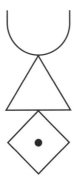

Seal of Cain

The sixth is named Cain, a young man whose heart is filled with resentment. Tears of frustration fall from his blind eye sockets as he stumbles on heavy limbs through the cosmic dance. His part of the heavens is Virgo, the Virgin.

Seal of Abel

The seventh is called Abel, brother to Cain. He laughs immoderately and spins lightly on his toes, his body slender and well balanced. He hates his brother for his ceaseless complaints and turns his back to him. His portion is Libra, the Balance.

Seal of Akiressina

The eighth is named Akiressina. Barbs that drip poison cover her naked limbs, and from the base of her spine coils a barbed tail ever ready to strike her unfortunate lovers. Her portion is Scorpio, the Scorpion.

Seal of Yubel

The ninth is called Yubel. In form he resembles the centaur, with four hoofed feet, but the lower part of his body is not that of a horse but of some alien creature that defies comparisons. His portion of the zodiac is Sagittarius, the Archer.

Seal of Harmupiael

The tenth is named Harmupiael. Silky white hairs cover his chest, and curling horns project from his head. His feet are cloven. His lustful part is Capricorn, the randy Goat.

Seal of Archiradonin

The eleventh is named Archiradonin. Alone among the dancing gods he has a body perfect in every detail, like that of a god of the Greeks, but he is without compassion. His portion is Aquarius, the Water Carrier.

Seal of Belias

The twelfth is called Belias. Her head is like that of a fish, arising from her shoulders directly, her fingers and toes are webbed for swimming, and her skin is blue and moist. Shining silver scales surround her breasts. Dark brown mottlings cover her back along her spine. Her portion is Pisces, the Fishes.

Throne of Chaos

Before the fall of Barbelzoa, the triple throne of creation was white, the pure color of milk. Azathoth sat upon the largest central seat arrayed in purple robes, with a crown of gold around his forehead. At his left hand sat his beautiful daughter Barbelzoa, with a silver crown on her brow. The right-hand seat supported only a spiked crown of black iron, for it was reserved for the future son of the goddess, destined to be engendered by her own father within her womb when she came into the ripeness of her maturity. Then the son would put on the iron crown and occupy the right-hand seat of the throne, as the daughter occupied the left-hand seat, and the harmony of heaven would attain its perfection.

So read the akashic records of the Old Ones, but they must be understood in a poetic way, for at the heart of creation, there are no material things as we understand them, but only the essences or ideals of things. The gods are described by the poets in ways that allow human comprehension. The mind of man cannot conceive their true shapes, which extend beyond our reality into higher and lower planes.

The throne of Azathoth was carved from a single block of white stone harder than the hardest marble, with sparks of fire dancing in its milky translucent depths, so that it seemed to burn with embers deep within. It occupied a high mount of irregular black basalt at the top of ninety-three wide steps cut into the living rock of the mount, the firmament above it surrounded by ceaselessly flickering coruscations of brilliant colors. At the base of the steps, the gatekeeper Yog-Sothoth filled the space within a pointed stone archway, his countenance turned outward, barring the transition of any soul unworthy to come before the wisdom seat and speak its own name for judgment.

The notes of Azathoth's unbroken flute made a sinuous rainbow upon the glowing air that surrounded the throne mount, and formed a pathway for the twelve archons to dance upon, who were then thirteen, for among their number was a pair of conjoined twins who were brother and sister. It is said that in those times Azathoth was not blind, and that the twelve who were thirteen could see like eagles all that passed in the countless worlds that filled the pit of stars below. They moderated their dance with compassion and judgment so that the cosmos was always balanced and well ordered.

In an open space beneath the central throne rested a scroll of white parchment on a roller of pure gold. Upon it were written the names of all those intelligent souls that had ascended through the ranks of successive births and rebirths to dwell in the summer land. They were not human souls, since humanity had yet to arise from the slime, but were souls of alien worlds. The summer land was the most perfect creation of the dancing gods, a place of sweet waters and lush green fields, with great forests filled with game beasts, and fields that never needed planting, but always brought forth their crops without fail. Without need to labor for bread, the souls occupied their minds with practice of the arts and the study of philosophy. Each time a new soul ascended to this summer land, a new name was added to the scroll, which was of endless length.

Chief among the dancing gods in beauty and intelligence was Nyarlathotep, who occupied the third place in the ring of heaven beside his twin sister Galila. They shared the same flesh, linked to each other at the side—Nyarlathotep was the left side and Galila the right side. In appearance Nyarlathotep was perfect of form and face, and keen in mind, whereas his sister was clumsy and dull, yet when Galila smiled, her brother glowered with rage, and when Galila sang songs of joy, her darkly beautiful half muttered curses.

Nyarlathotep grew weary of heaven. He found its perfect harmonies tedious and chafed at his subservience to Azathoth. He looked down upon the chaos mount and lusted after Barbelzoa. He used his necromancy to cast a sleep that was like death over the All-Father and his child. Azathoth slumbered, yet all the while he continued to pipe the music of his flute, which can never cease while he endures, for were the music to cease, all the myriad worlds would end.

While Azathoth slept and dreamed upon the white throne, Nyarlathotep descended from his place, tearing his flesh away from the side of Galila, who cried out in agony so that the heavens shook. He caught the sleeping goddess up in his arms and raped her. This is not to be understood of the body, but in another manner of the spirit. When she awoke and saw what he had done, in shame she threw herself into the endless pit of stars and fell down and down for countless ages, wrapping her shining body ever tighter around herself as its outer shell turned to hard stone, and making salt seas upon its surface with her never-ending tears.

When Azathoth cast off his unnatural sleep and saw that she had abandoned her place on the throne mount, he went mad with grief. He put out his own eyes with his fingernails, rent his purple robes, and cast away his golden crown. His flute cracked and the triple throne turned black as jet. The endless day around the throne transformed into endless night. What had been the towering heights of heaven became the deepest pit of chaos, the center of a world-consuming vortex that ate both space and time.

The eyes of the dancing gods were put out at the same moment Azathoth struck himself blind, all but those of Nyarlathotep who had divided himself from the twelve. Their dance faltered, for the music was no longer perfect in its rhythms. Evolved souls from the myriads of worlds ceased to present themselves before the arch of Yog-Sothoth to plead admission to the throne mount. Blind Azathoth squatted in his seat, neglected in his own filth and drool. In disgust, Nyarlathotep assumed control over the blackened throne. He placed the iron crown upon his head and sat in the right-hand seat that had been reserved for the first-born son of Azathoth, administering the mute will of Azathoth.

He removed the golden scroll from beneath the central throne. From between the very legs of Azathoth he took it. Never before had any other dared to touch the scroll. In fury he rent it into fragments and scattered them throughout the cosmos. These fragments became all the truths in all the worlds that are known to some but not to others. The perfect summer land of realized souls was transformed into a dark hell of torment and hunger. Those trapped within it shall never be released until Barbelzoa is restored to her seat at the left hand of her father, with a male child of promise engendered in her womb.

Nyarlathotep made a black book, and into it he inscribed the laws of chaos, and the names of souls who pledge their worship and service to him for eternity. It is called the *Necronomicon*, or Book of the Laws of the Dead, for all whose names are written within it are dead to their former earthly lives, though they yet walk. The book by the poet of Yemen, Abdul Alhazred, is only an echo of this black book of dead names. There are many false books but only one true *Necronomicon*. In his blindness and idiocy, Azathoth is not even aware that the book rests beneath him.

Nyarlathotep longs to strike the naked Azathoth from the central seat of the triple throne and wash it clean of filth so that he can take his place there, but does not dare interrupt the music of the flute, for when the music stops, all things will cease to be as if they had never been. He cannot seize the throne by force. The Crawling Chaos schemes for ways to restore the goddess Barbelzoa to the throne mount so that he can compel her to become his queen and engender a child in her womb. In that way he will claim the golden crown for his own by right of succession. In union with the goddess lies his path to ultimate ascendancy.

The throne of Azathoth is the seat of power, and all power flows from it. Only when the goddess is restored to her place on the left-hand seat shall there be harmony again in heaven, and the dark mourning of Azathoth be lifted from the cosmos. Nyarlathotep will seize all power to himself, and reward his worshippers and servants with rich gifts. The old god and his flute he will relegate to the smaller right-hand seat that he once occupied, and will take the central throne for his own. All restraints will fall from him. He will make and destroy worlds at will.

Yet before this can occur, he must wipe this globe clean of all lower forms of life, so that it can be lifted back up to its former place by his servants, the Old Ones, and by those transformed among our race who aid his purpose. Those who do his bidding are granted precious favors, and magic is theirs to command. It may be long ages before the stars come right, and the Old Ones walk unhindered across the land. Nyarlathotep seeks to speed the cleansing of this world by having the Old Ones engender a race of hybrids on mortal women, but the work is slow. Those who serve him enjoy rare pleasures while this work goes forward over many lifetimes. In the end of days, they will be lifted up and a suitable reward found for them. In the meanwhile, they thrive and work their will on this ignorant mass of man, who know nothing of the change that is to come, apart from a few vague myths they refuse to credit.

BOOK OF THE EAST GATE:
FOUNDATION

Sacred Space

There is a division of the Old Ones in this fallen world that came about some six hundred million years ago. One clan consists of those who formerly inhabited windowless cities of black basalt on the surface of this globe, but were driven beneath the earth by the Great Race from Yith into tunnels and vast caverns unknown to man, where they reside still, waiting for the stars to come right in the heavens before emerging.

The other clan of the Old Ones never dwelt on the surface at all, but lived in the sky amid dimensions of space, and found access to this reality through the gateway of Yog-Sothoth. There they remain, behind the gate, unable to come bodily down to this world because of the poisonous pattern of stars that now persists, but will one day pass away. Men communicate with them through rituals on those angular days of the year when the gaps between worlds narrow, and the walls that separate realities thin.

The Old Ones below the earth have little interest in the affairs of men. It is possible to communicate with them by conducting rites of propitiation or sacrifice in deep places such as caves, mines, tunnels, pits, hollows, valleys, cellars, basements, and wells. They are invoked up from the bowels of the ground, which forms no barrier to their passage, for they are not of the same substance as mortal life. Wards of magic alone can bar their passage, such as are inscribed on the great doors that seal their dark tunnels. Necromancers seek commerce with these chthonic Old Ones and use the things of the earthen element and its symbols to draw them up. The shades of the dead may be invoked to speak for the Old Ones as their messengers, since these deep-dwelling gods have affinity for all things dead and rotting. Seals, charms, and talismans to be empowered by them are buried in soil at the center of a hallowed space, or placed beneath stone.

The Old Ones who dwell upon the heights of the air have long held commerce with wizards. They are invoked in high places such as towers, tall buildings, roof-tops, attics, upper rooms of houses, hilltops, and mountain peaks. In ancient times, they were called down into stone circles on the crowns of hills. So it is still done by those wise in the ways of magic, for the old places retain their power even though the standing stones have fallen or cracked with frost. The open air is best to call upon the Old Ones of the heights, but when concealment from other men is necessary for the sake of prudence, a roofed chamber will serve. They are invoked with face and eyes elevated, and chants sent into the heavens, for the gate of Yog-Sothoth opens from above.

The sacred space for invocation of the dwellers in the heights requires an open ground or floor to accommodate the circle of art. When standing in the center of the space, it is enough for the rites of a single mage, or a pair of companions in the art, to be able to walk three paces in all of the four directions. Those who must use a smaller chamber will be restricted in movement around the altar, but this is not a fatal hindrance in itself. A resolute will and nimble wit overcome all obstacles to success.

The rites of the Old Ones are not for the eyes and ears of the uninitiated. Those who spy upon high magic corrupt it, causing misfortune to themselves and to others. A place must be chosen that is secure from intrusion, where the words of chants cannot be distinguished. Keep it separate and apart for the works of wizardry, and bar the entry of unbelievers for their own well-being. The very air of the sacred space becomes charged with potency, and provokes evil dreams, unease, and waking visions in those who breathe it. When the Old Ones come, the gate of Yog-Sothoth gapes like a hungry mouth. It is not a place for fools.

Stone Circle

The sacred circle of the Old Ones is formed from seven well-chosen stones, each of a size that can without great difficulty be carried in two hands, so that the circle is not fixed into place but may be moved at will. This enables its concealment should its place of working be discovered, and its removal and erection at another place. The stones are arrayed on the ground, or the floor of the chamber of art, in a great circle that is large enough to accommodate the altar, with sufficient space to walk around the altar yet remain within the bounds of the circle. They are equally divided, so that a line drawn upon the earth from stone to stone would form a regular star of seven points.

Understand that the true circle of art is erected in the astral world, where all magic is worked. The ring of stones is used to fix the location, size, and shape of the astral circle. When the magician enters the astral realm in his imagination, the stones must be conceived as large and standing upright, just as the sacred space itself must be visualized as on a high hill or at the top of a tower. In the usual course of working, invocation is made only to the Old Ones of the upper airs, since those of the pits are at best indifferent to human intentions, and at their worst, actively malicious. All of the lords are invoked through the gates of Yog-Sothoth, which form about the circle upon the air.

In the choosing of the stones for the circle, there is no invariable guide. The magician looks deep into his heart and listens to the candidate stone. If it speaks to him in the mind, it will speak with the voice of one of the seven lords of the Old Ones, and forever after it will be the stone of that god. The stone may not use words to speak, but may express the nature of the lord of the Old Ones with which it resonates mutely, as a kind of humming that is felt in the bones of the head.

It is best if the stones of the lords are colored in the hues that accord with the celestial spheres of the lords. Naturally-colored stones are to be preferred, but the inner resonance of the stone is more important than its color. Natural colors of stones are seldom intense, but are more easily visible when the stone is moistened with water. If the necromancer has difficulty locating seven appropriate stones of different colors, stones of the same kind may be stained or painted over their surfaces in the colors of the seven lords. These are the colors:

Azathoth (Sunday): yellow
Dagon (Monday): purple
Cthulhu (Tuesday): red
Nyarlathotep (Wednesday): orange
Yog-Sothoth (Thursday): blue
Shub-Niggurath (Friday): green
Yig (Saturday): black

The seven stones are laid out in a circle so that they rest on the points of an invisible star, each stone according with a planetary sphere and with a day of the week associated with that sphere. The stone of Yig is aligned with the direction of the north. Following the clock, their order around the circle is: Yig (Saturn), Yog-Sothoth (Jupiter), Cthulhu (Mars), Azathoth (Sun), Shub-Niggurath (Venus), Nyarlathotep (Mercury), Dagon (Moon). Proceed around the circle clockwise and you have the order of the planets in the heavens from slowest and most distant to quickest and nearest. Follow the reflecting line of the star clockwise, and you have the order of the days of the week.

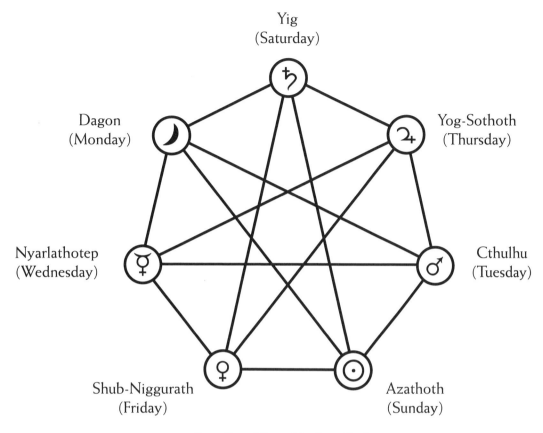

Yig
(Saturday)

Yog-Sothoth
(Thursday)

Dagon
(Monday)

Cthulhu
(Tuesday)

Nyarlathotep
(Wednesday)

Shub-Niggurath
(Friday)

Azathoth
(Sunday)

Seven-Rayed Star of the Stone Circle

The ordering of the planets is based upon their apparent movement through the heavens, as observed from the surface of the earth by ancient astrologers, who believed the earth to be the center of the universe. They mistook the sun and moon for planets, because these great lights appeared to move in much the same way as the five true planets visible with the naked eye. By applying the planetary spheres to the points of the heptagram, the ordering of the days of the week, which are associated with the planets, was derived.

It is not necessary to draw or mark upon the ground or floor of the sacred space the star of seven points. The star is used as a device for remembering the correct order of the stones, and for placing them accurately around the circle of art. Nor is it required that you draw a circle, although it is easier to place the stones regularly when a circle is traced lightly into the floor or ground of the place of working. It is the stones themselves that create the physical foundation for the circle, not lines marked on the floor.

The method of placing the stones at the same distance from the center of the circle is easy to tell. Obtain a cord or rope and cut it to the same length as the radius of the circle you desire. This will depend on the constraints of your sacred space, but three paces is a good length, although if necessary it may be longer or shorter. Fasten one end of this cord down in the center of the space, using a pin, a nail, the point of a dagger, or, if it is desirable that the floor not be marred, a heavy weight that will hold the end securely. Then extend the cord toward the north and place the stone of Yig at the end of the cord. Move the cord one-seventh part of the circumference of the circle clockwise and place at its end the stone of Yog-Sothoth. Continue in this manner around the circle to place the remaining stones.

A circle lightly inscribed on the ground or floor of the sacred space will aid in the equal spacing of the stones, but it is unessential. Small variations in the spacing will not prove fatal to successful rites in honor of the lords of the Old Ones. Strive to make the arrangement of the circle as harmonious as possible. Any gross distortion in the circle, or large gap in the spacing of the stones, will create a weak point in the ring of stones on the astral level, and may have unfortunate consequences. It may allow the occult energy raised to leak away from the circle, rendering a ritual ineffective. It may even allow the intrusion of an unwelcome intelligence into the circle, to vex the attention of the magician. The more regular the ring of stones, the stronger its barrier to contain or repel.

The Altar

The true altar is built up upon the astral plane using an image in the mind of the physical altar, which acts as a solid foundation to define the location, form, and size of the astral altar. The material components of the altar consist of three candlesticks with candles inset in their sockets, and three flat rods of wood, each one yard in length.

The wooden slats are painted in the ancient planetary colors of the three higher lords of the Old Ones: Azathoth (yellow), Nyarlathotep (orange), Yog-Sothoth (blue). They are flat to prevent them from rolling when laid upon the ground or floor. A common wooden yardstick makes an ideal rod. In place of candles, small oil lamps may be used—it is only essential that three living flames burn on the altar. The glass shades of lamps have the advantage of shielding the flames from random currents of air stirred by the working of rituals.

In the center of the circle of seven stones, arrange the three rods in a triangle upon the ground or floor of the sacred space, so that one point of the triangle is directed to the north. Standing behind the triangle and facing north, the yellow rod of Azathoth forms its right side, the orange rod of Nyarlathotep its left side, and the blue rod of Yog-Sothoth the base of the triangle of the altar. Inside each of the points of the triangle set one of the candle holders or lamps, which should be all of the same kind and size. Short, circular brass candlesticks are suitable. If oil lamps are used, they should be small and round.

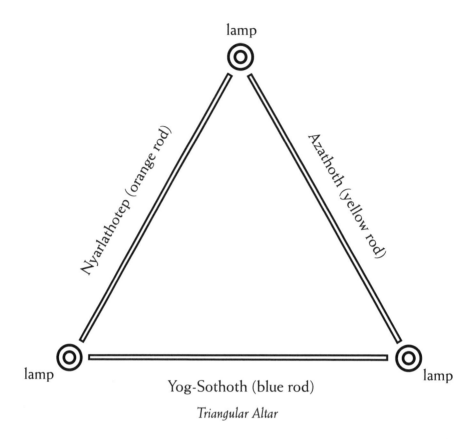

Triangular Altar

The altar locates the invisible gate of Yog-Sothoth, which forms high above the altar at the center of the stone circle. All power descends into the circle through this gate. All chants rise from the circle through the gate above the altar. The direction of space given to Yog-Sothoth is the direction of the heights. There are six other gates, but they are all extensions of Yog-Sothoth, for this lord is the sole gatekeeper. Offerings and sacrifices are placed within the bounds of the altar, which is the space within the circle given over wholly to the Old Ones and their lords for material interactions with them. Charms and talismans are charged within the triangle. The tools of the rites are placed on the altar when not in use.

A small sitting mat may be placed for comfort at the southern side of the altar, next to the blue rod of Yog-Sothoth. When not walking the circle, or standing before its gates and stones, the magician works seated on the mat, facing the north. If he shares the rites with a companion, she will sit on a similar mat in the north, facing south, so that the altar is between them. The mats should be flat so that they may be easily walked across without tripping the feet. The sitting posture is useful for meditation and astral projection.

The candles should be of the same size and shape. If they can be obtained, use a yellow, a blue, and an orange candle in the points of the altar triangle, setting them by color so that they are opposite the rods of the same color. The blue candle of Yog-Sothoth is place in the north point, the yellow candle of Azathoth is placed in the westerly point on the left, and the orange candle of Nyarlathotep is placed in the easterly point on the right. If candles of the appropriate colors cannot be found, use white candles for all three points of the altar. The colors of the candles do not affect the colors of the flames, but they have a resonance with the three high lords. Those who employ transparent glass oil lamps may, if they wish, add a drop of food coloring to the clear oil of each lamp.

Candles or lamps within the points of the altar should be lit before the start of the rite in ordered sequence, beginning with the point of the north and moving counterclockwise, which is the chaotic direction of rotation. They are extinguished after the end of the rite in reverse order. If there is more than one present in the circle, the master of the rite lights and extinguishes the candles. As many as seven may share the rite within the bounds of a large stone circle, spacing their places around the altar so that they are evenly separated from each other, but if more wish to be present, they should observe the rite from outside the circle, and may lend their voices to the chants.

The Gates

The four outer gates are flat rods of wood one yard in length that are laid upon the ground, or the floor, of the sacred space in the four directions of the compass. These rods represent the thresholds of gateways in the four watchtowers of this world. To step across these thresholds in the astral body is to pass through the gates. Those things from outside can be called inside to stand before the circle of stones in their astral shapes. The mind of the magician can be projected outside the bounds of common space through the gates in any of the four directions.

The rod of the north gate is colored black and accords with Yig and his works. The rod of the east gate is colored green and accords with Shub-Niggurath and her works. The rod of the south gate is colored red and accords with Cthulhu and his works. The rod of the west gate is colored purple and accords with Dagon and his works.

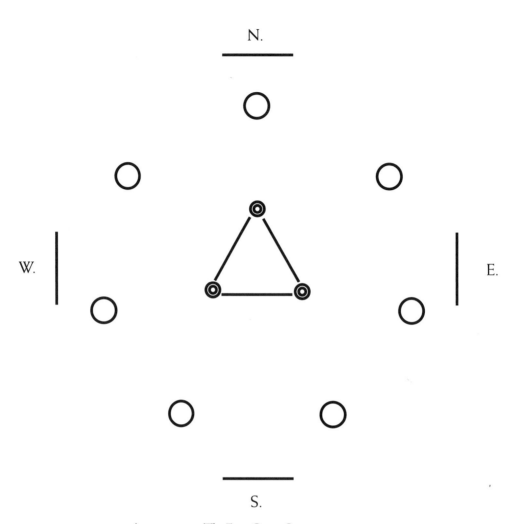

The Four Outer Gates

To step across the thresholds at the four quarters is to travel in the astral body to those lands that lie beyond the bounds of the watchtowers of this world. Transition can only be made through a gate that has been opened by Yog-Sothoth. All gates are sealed until Yog-Sothoth opens them. Yog-Sothoth is the gatekeeper to the outer gates, and to the inner gates.

The rods of the gates should be aligned with the walls of the ritual chamber, if the rites of the Old Ones are conducted beneath a roof, and may be placed flush against the baseboards of those four walls, if the working space is limited. It will usually be the case that the four walls of the chamber do not face the four directions of space in a precise way. Each wall that is most aligned with a direction should be assumed to face that direction. The wall that most nearly lies in the east should be termed the east wall, and the rod of the east gate place against it or somewhat in front of it, even if it is not aligned exactly to the east. So for the other three walls.

When conducting the rites beneath the stars, a compass may be used to determine north, and the four gates laid accordingly at an equal distance from the stone circle. Magnetic north should be used rather than true north, since the magnetic lines of force that span the body of the earth are aligned in this way, and are the living energies of the sleeping goddess.

Where a formal temple of the Old Ones is established, banners of the gates may be hung on the walls of the chamber behind and above the threshold rods. Each banner shall consist of a background that is colored the color of the opposite gate, with the seal of the banner gate centered upon it in the color of that gate. The banner of the gateway of the north is red with the seal of Yig large upon it in black. The banner of the gateway of the east is purple with the seal of Shub-Niggurath in green. The banner of the gateway of the south is black with the seal of Cthulhu in red. The banner of the gateway of the west is green with the seal of Dagon in purple.

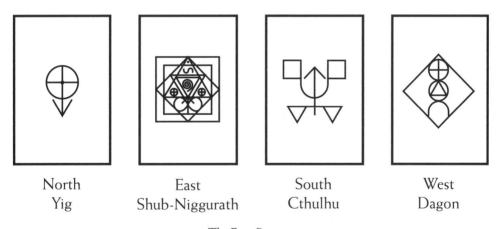

| North | East | South | West |
| Yig | Shub-Niggurath | Cthulhu | Dagon |

The Four Banners

The banners shall be twenty-two inches across by thirty-three inches in length, with the seals large and centered upon them. The background material may be of paper, parchment, textiles, or whichever material is most convenient for the magician. Banners of cloth may be hung from portable wooden or metal racks on stands when it is desired to erect them in an open space where they must stand freely. But in an enclosed chamber of the art, the banners may be of any convenient material and may be hung or otherwise fastened to the four walls of the chamber, centered at the level of the heart of the magician who uses the circle or leads the use of the circle.

The four outer gates open outward through the watchtowers at the far corners of this world, but the three inner gates lie concealed within the center of being, and lead inward to the source of creation along the axis of the world. The upper gate belongs to Yog-Sothoth, the lower gate to Nyarlathotep, and the central gate to Azathoth, who resides at the center of everything. The four lower lords rule the outer gates, the three higher lords rule the inner gates, and Yog-Sothoth controls all their openings and shuttings, obedient to the music played on the flute of the idiot god, Azathoth. Nyarlathotep is the messenger who bears communications through all the gates, and who shows the astral traveler the ways that lie beyond them.

The Keys

To each lord of the Old Ones is given a key for the rites of adoration and petition. When a lord is honored in the daily rite, the key of that lord is placed in the center of the altar. By repeated use, the keys acquire power to catch the awareness of the lords they represent. Through the keys the force of the magician's will may be directed at the lords, and at any lesser spirits of the Old Ones commanded in the names of the lords.

Yig: lemniscate
Yog-Sothoth: circle
Cthulhu: trapezoid
Azathoth: spiral
Shub-Niggurath: triangle
Nyarlathotep: rod
Dagon: crescent

It is the geometric shapes of the keys that are most significant, not the materials from which the keys are made, or their colors. Rods or straps of mild steel are a good medium for the keys, although brass is better because it gives forth a purer ringing tone when struck upon the stones of the circle. The keys should be durable enough to handle daily without distortions of their shapes, and all of approximately the same overall size. From six to nine inches across in their longest dimension is manageable in the hand. It is convenient to bend them from single lengths of steel or brass rods, or flat steel or brass strapping that can be bent easily over the edge of an anvil with a hammer. The rod or strapping used must be thick enough to hold its shape in use, and to give forth a ringing when held loosely between the fingers and struck on the stones.

Each key will give forth its own unique tone, because each is different in shape. The gap in the outline of each key is necessary to allow the rod that composes the key to vibrate freely, so that its voice can be heard during rituals. It is not necessary that the ringing of the keys be loud, so long as a distinct sound is produced when the keys are struck lightly on the stones. If necessary, the keys can be suspended in the hand from loops of twine, to allow them to vibrate more freely and produce a more ringing tone when struck, but if they are well made and held loosely between the fingers, this should not be necessary. Brass keys will ring better than steel keys, but heavy steel rods or strappings will also work well.

It is not necessary to paint these keys since it is the outline of their geometric forms that gives them their identities. However, if desired for aesthetic reasons, they may all be painted the same flat black to conceal irregularities and imperfections and to make them uniform in appearance. A rust-resistant paint intended to cover metal should be used for the sake of durability.

Lemniscate of Yig

The lemniscate of Yig has the shape of an elongated figure eight turned on its side, and represents the infinite starry void beyond the sphere of Saturn. The lemniscate is the symbol of infinity. Conceive of it as a great serpent with its tail held in its jaws, its body forming a loop that crosses upon itself.

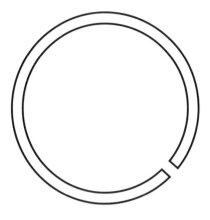

Circle of Yog-Sothoth

The circle of Yog-Sothoth represents the cosmic gateway of the god, and for this reason is open at the center, so that it takes the shape of a flat hoop. It represents the circle of the zodiac, which demarcates the sphere of the fixed stars and the gateway to the higher spheres.

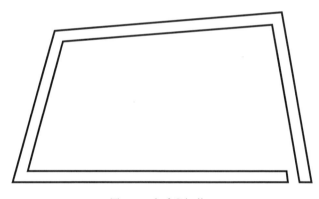

Trapezoid of Cthulhu

The trapezoid of Cthulhu expresses the alien geometry of the great stone doorway that seals the house of Cthulhu on sunken R'lyeh, where there are no right angles. Bend the rod that forms it so that each of its four angles is different from the other three, and none of them are ninety degrees. This irregular figure is known as a trapezium.

Spiral of Azathoth

The spiral of Azathoth stands for the vortex at the center of chaos, where the blind idiot god Azathoth squats upon his black throne, piping his cracked flute. It winds inward three and one-half turns in a counterclockwise direction.

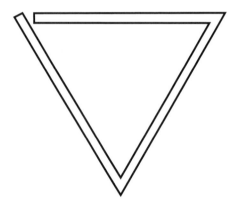

Triangle of Shub-Niggurath

The inverted triangle of Shub-Niggurath symbolizes the sexual triangle of the vulva that is outlined in female pubic hair, and is sometimes referred to as the delta of Venus. When holding it, always orient it so that its point is downward. However, understand that Shub-Niggurath contains inherent in her nature both male and female sexuality, and the triangle can easily be turned so that its point is upward.

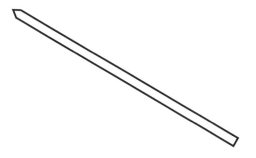

Rod of Nyarlathotep

The rod of Nyarlathotep is a symbol of authority, which this god has from Azathoth on the black throne of chaos as the soul and messenger of the twelve dancing gods. It is made from heavy rod or strapping, with one end filed or ground into a triangular point. This directs the flow of force outward from the point and suggests unbalanced force, for the judgments of Nyarlathotep are never impartial.

Crescent of Dagon

The crescent of Dagon stands for the moon and her sway over the tides and life cycles of the seas. It can be used to represent both a benevolent waxing crescent, or a baneful waning crescent, depending on how it is held in the hand—when held with both points upright it is understood to be waxing, but with both points downward, it is presumed to be waning.

Ritual Apparel

It is desirable but not essential that those who observe the rites of the seven lords of the Old Ones in the stone circle of art possess a black robe. The blackness of the robe represents the darkness of primordial chaos surrounding the throne of Azathoth, as well as the inner darkness of the blind gods, who see by another sense than vision. The sleeves of the robes should be loose and extend to at least the mid-forearm, but no lower than the wrist, and the hem should be at least to the mid-calf but no lower than the ankle. The robes may be hooded or without hoods, but a magician who works the rites with a temple group should wear robes that match those of his companions.

Comfortable clothing of neutral black is to be worn beneath the robes for all rites. The necromancer may go barefoot, or if footwear is required due to the rough ground during outdoor rites, he should wear simple shoes of black canvas that are worn on no other occasions. Similarly, the black clothing worn beneath the robes should be reserved for ritual work. If no robe is available, they serve as the outer ritual garments. Jewelry should be removed before the start of the rite, but it is not necessary to remove rings difficult to get off the fingers, or jewelry that pierces through the skin.

Sashes of silk or a similar fine fabric are to be worn around the waist, brightly hued in the color of the lord for which the daily rite is conducted. The sash ties the black robe closed, or if no robe is used, ties around the black ritual garb at the waist. Seven sashes for the seven lords—black for Yig, blue for Yog-Sothoth, red for Cthulhu, yellow for Azathoth, green for Shub-Niggurath, orange for Nyarlathotep, and purple for Dagon.

Each sash shall be as broad as the breadth of the hand of the disciple who wears it, and in length the measure of his height from the soles of the feet to the crown of the head. It is tied in front on the waist above the left thigh and its ends permitted to hang free.

There are three ranks in the Order of the Old Ones, as it is here established— Servant, Master, and Lord. Servants wear the symbol of the key of Yog-Sothoth, which is the blue circle, embroidered, sewn or otherwise attached to the left breast of their black robes. Masters add above this symbol the pointed orange rod of Nyarlathotep so that it points upward and away from the blue circle of Yog-Sothoth, to show their higher rank. Lords add the yellow spiral of Azathoth above the point of the rod of Nyarlathotep to indicate the third and highest rank of the Order.

Servant   Master   Lord

Emblems of Rank

In addition to the black robe and the sash in the color of the lord of the daily rite that is being conducted, the magician shall wear on a chain, cord, or ribbon around his neck a lamen bearing the seal of the lord of the rite, so that the lamen hangs over his chest at the level of his heart. A lamen is a pendant bearing the seal of a god or other potent spiritual being. Each lamen is three inches in diameter and circular in shape. On the face of the lamens, the background color for all seven of the seals is white, the color of all seven of the seals themselves is black. Upon the back of each lamen, the sigil of its lord is inscribed in black on a white background. The sigils are extracted from the names of the lords upon the magic squares of the lords.

Each lamen is rimmed around its edge with the color of the lord of the Old Ones to which it corresponds. The lamen of Yig is rimmed in black, that of Yog-Sothoth in blue, that of Cthulhu in red, that of Azathoth in yellow, that of Shub-Niggurath in green, that of Nyarlathotep in orange, and that of Dagon in purple.

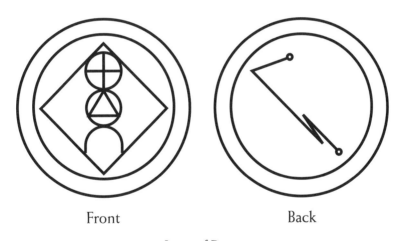

Front   Back

Lamen of Dagon

The lamens may be made of flat disks of metal or wood, painted on both faces. Another way to make the lamens of the seven lords is to obtain seven matching round wooden picture frames of small diameter, and set an eyehook into the top of each frame so that it may be hung around the neck on a ribbon or chain. The seals can then be painted or marked in black on disks of white parchment or white paper, with the sigils marked in black on the opposite side, and inserted into the round picture frames behind the glass. The sigils on the backs of the paper disks will not be visible, but will still be effective. The wooden frames may then be painted in the colors that match the lords of the seals.

Those who have been elevated to the rank of Master, and who make a choice of one of the seven ways of approach to the throne of chaos, wear an emblem that indicates to the other members of the Order which path they have chosen to walk. They wear this both while learning the discipline of their chosen lord, and after they have succeeded in attaining the black throne. It is worn in an exposed place where it will be easily visible, but it is not worn with ostentation as a vain display. It is a badge of devotion that binds the wearer to the way of the lord it represents. The emblem may be an actual physical object or a representation of that object in the form of jewelry or a decoration.

The emblem of Yig is a knotted cord or noose, or else brooch, pin, or bracelet bearing the form of a knotted cord or noose. The emblem of Shub-Niggurath is a rose, or a piece of jewelry bearing the form of a rose. Cthulhu the warrior has the knife as his emblem, or a representation of a knife or sword in the form of jewelry. Dagon has as his emblem the book or scroll, or its representation in miniature. The emblem of Yog-Sothoth is a key or the miniature decorative representation of a key. The emblem of Nyarlathotep is a human skull or its representation in jewelry. Azathoth has for his emblem a whistle or flute, or a piece of jewelry in this shape.

The Marks

Those who walk one of the seven paths of the lords in their quest for the attainment of the black throne may wish to adopt the seal of that lord as a body marking, in token of the fidelity that is owed to that lord. The use of the seal as a tattoo is voluntary. The seal of Yig marks the path of the north gate, the seal of Shub-Niggurath the path of the east gate, the seal of Cthulhu the path of the south gate, the seal of Dagon the path of the west gate, the seal of Yog-Sothoth the path of the upper gate, the seal of Nyarlathotep the path of the lower gate, and the seal of Azathoth the path of the central gate which alone among the seven paths has no duration or extent.

The seal chosen is impressed into the skin as a sign of respect and fidelity to the lord of the Old Ones whose name it invokes. It binds the wearer to that lord, and is not to be adopted lightly, for there is potency in the very shape and strokes that compose it. Consider long which lord you choose as your mentor on the quest for the black throne. The tattoo of the seal should be placed on the body with dignity. Among the appropriate places on the body are the base of the neck, the small of the back, the left breast above the heart, and the inside of the left forearm.

Tattoos should be made in black ink. Colors should not be used. The size is a matter for the discretion of the disciple, but it should not exceed an area that can be covered by the palm of the hand. The mark of the lord of the path is to be worn with respect. It is not required for the magic and rites of the Old Ones, but those who have committed themselves on one of the seven paths of attainment may wish to formalize their decision by accepting the mark of their chosen lord. Such marks are not decorations. Only one of the seven should be adopted, and only by the magician who has searched into his or her heart, and has made irrevocable commitment to the path, for once a path is walked, it cannot be unwalked.

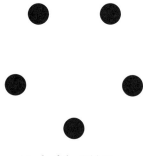

Mark of the Old Ones

As a general sign of membership in the esoteric Order of the Old Ones, the mark of the Old Ones may be tattooed on the skin in whatever place is most convenient. It is useful to place the mark where it can be displayed easily to others, as an informal significator of membership in the Order. The mark is a miniature version of the footprint of the Old Ones, which has been left by their unseen passage in sand and in dust. It is composed of five identical black dots arranged on the points of an invisible pentalpha that expresses the five virtues of Attention, Ardor, Aggression, Authority, and Attainment.

The mark of the Old Ones should always be quite small. It is not for decorative display, but is a sign of devotion to the purposes of the Old Ones and membership in their esoteric Order. Those who take upon themselves the mark of five points pledge themselves to study the ways of the Old Ones through their seven lords, and to aid the Old Ones in their great work of restoring the earth to her rightful place on the triple throne of chaos, at the left hand of Azathoth. This is a noble service, for by its fulfillment the order and harmony of the cosmos, lost in the madness of Azathoth since the fall of Barbelzoa, shall be reestablished.

The Seal Disks

The lords of the Old Ones are capricious and quick to anger. This is especially true of Nyarlathotep, who will as often injure those who seek his attention as he will benefit them. It may be necessary to seek protection from the aroused wrath of one of the lords. This is accomplished by means of the Elder Seal, which has power over all the Old Ones, both outer lords and inner lords, even over great Nyarlathotep. It was created by the Elder Things as a weapon against the Old Ones. Great is the power of the Old Ones, but greater still was the wisdom of the Elder Things.

By its segments and angles, the Elder Seal mimics and evokes the same poisonous but invisible rays that are cast down from the malefic alignment of the stars. Its force is more concentrated than that of the stars in the heavens, so that even Nyarlathotep, who can walk abroad beneath the moon when wrapped about in his black robes and veiled across the face, finds it difficult to confront the Elder Seal. The sentient things that were made by the Old Ones, and that still dwell in the deep places of the earth, or between the stars, suffer the same pain when the seal is exposed to them.

The Elder Seal

Paint the Elder Seal in gold upon both sides of a black disk that is five inches across. The seal will function potently even when all its details are not precisely rendered, for in its relationships of angles and lengths of rays force is compounded and reinforced, so that a part of the seal has the potency of its entirety.

The Elder Seal should be placed on the altar, between the three lights, during all rites of the Old Ones, but should always be carefully wrapped in white cloth and tied closed with white cord, so that no portion of it is exposed to the sight. If during the course of any rite, the life or sanity of the magician is threatened, the Elder Seal may be unwrapped and used to ward off the threat. Under no circumstances should it be left exposed during normal rites of worship, since its exposed face will prevent the approach of the lords and their servants, and will negate the working of the rites.

The temptation is strong to unleash the Elder Seal to command and compel to obedience the minions of the lords, or even the lords themselves. This temptation should be denied. The Old Ones are not to be trifled with. Magicians who think that the lords can be commanded learn their error in sorrow. The Old Ones favor those who serve them, but they never forget a transgression, and they never forgive. Use the Elder Seal in defense of your sanity and your life, but for no lesser reason.

Each of the twelve dancing gods has a seal that is used to represent the god in the solemn Rite of the Dancing Gods that is conducted on the nights of the equinox, but the seals are also employed when individual dancing gods are invoked for ritual purposes that fall into their zones of authority. These seals are painted or otherwise delineated in black on the front side of white disks of wood or metal three inches in diameter. On the reverse side of each disk is marked in black the zodiac sign which that god corresponds. The rims of the disks are colored in the color of the lord of the Old Ones who is the active agent for that dancing god. The seal disks of the dancing gods resemble the lamens of the seven lords, but the seals of the twelve gods are not worn around the neck, and have no loop or hook by which they may be hung from a chain.

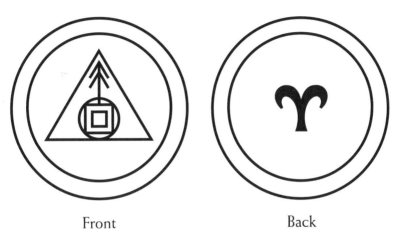

Front   Back

Seal Disk of Athoth

The following list indicates which zodiac sign is associated with each of the twelve gods, and should be marked on the reverse of the seal disk, and which lord's color should be painted around the rim.

Athoth (Aries): red of Cthulhu (Mars)

Harmas (Taurus): green of Shub-Niggurath (Venus)

Galila (Gemini): orange of Nyarlathotep (Mercury)

Yobel (Cancer): purple of Dagon (Moon)

Adonaios (Leo): yellow of Azathoth (Sun)

Cain (Virgo): orange of Nyarlathotep (Mercury)

Abel (Libra): green of Shub-Niggurath (Venus)

Akiressina (Scorpio): red of Cthulhu (Mars)

Yubel (Sagittarius): blue of Yog-Sothoth (Jupiter)

Harmupiael (Capricorn): black of Yig (Saturn)
Archiradonin (Aquarius): black of Yig (Saturn)
Belias (Pisces): blue of Yog-Sothoth (Jupiter)

As the planets of the heavens rule the signs of the zodiac, so are the seven lords linked with the twelve dancing gods. However, it would be wrong to state that the lords rule the gods. They are active agents in natural harmony with the blind forces of the gods to which they are linked. Each lord draws upon the forces of two dancing gods, with the exception of Dagon, who is linked only with Yobel, and Azathoth, who is linked only with Adonaios. Through the gates and across the thresholds of the seven lords, by the authority of their names, the magician is able to invoke the blind forces of the dancing gods for works of magic.

Invoke Athoth for matters of self-growth and development, Harmas with regard to matters of security and the protection of possessions, Galila in affairs that concern the home and personal surroundings, Yobel in dealings of family or ownership, Adonaios in matters of creative expression and recreational activities, Cain in matters of personal health and service to others, Abel about affairs of partnerships and marriage, Akiressina in dealings with death and shared resources, Yubel about travel and communication, Harmupiael about career goals and social status, Archiradonin about social relationships and community activities, and Belias in matters of required duty or a troubled conscience.

The spheres of human activity recognized in astrology as under the influence of the twelve zodiac signs and their associated houses of the heavens shall be your guide in determining which of the twelve dancing gods should be invoked for any specific task. Invoke them and direct them in the names and by the authority of their lords, using the keys of the lords as tokens of that authority. In unique rituals for specific practical purposes that fall under the dancing gods, the key of the lord directs and impels the seal disk of the god, and both should be present on the altar ready for use at the commencement of such rituals.

The Necronomicon

No man has ever seen the true *Necronomicon*, but only an astral semblance of it that is a mere shadow of the reality. The book resides beneath the throne of Azathoth, the naked sight of which would tear the human mind to gibbering fragments. Its pages are infinite in number. On them is written in the language of the Old Ones the laws of chaos, and the names of those men, women, and alien beings who have pledged their lives in service to the great work of the Old Ones, the purging of the lands and seas of this earth of all vulgar life, and her elevation through the highest gate of Yog-Sothoth to the black throne. Only creatures that burrow deep beneath the skin of this world, or whose consciousness resembles that of the Old Ones themselves, will survive the transition and be released living before the throne when Barbelzoa regains her true form. Many of them will perish. Those that can endure the maelstrom of chaos may find themselves bound in service to Nyarlathotep and his unwilling bride Barbelzoa for eternity.

It is not the intention of Nyarlathotep that chaos should cease to dominate the universe. He has little wish for a return to the harmony of the golden age that was before the fall, but revels in the ceaseless fountain of disorder and all its wild outpourings. However, Yog-Sothoth has always preferred reason and the rule of law, and has always given his first allegiance to Azathoth, for he remembers the blind idiot god as he was before the descent of Barbelzoa into matter. Among the lords of the Old Ones, some there are such as Cthulhu who will side with the Crawling Chaos, but others such as Yig will support Yog-Sothoth. Nor is it certain which way the allegiance of all four of the other lords will turn, although some claim that Yog-Sothoth has the sympathy of Dagon. Neither man nor god can predict what will happen when the princess is restored to her left-hand seat on the triple throne.

Nyarlathotep has promised to transform the elect among his followers on the earth so that their minds and bodies become able to withstand the torments of chaos. The *Necronomicon* states that this transition to higher space will not be long in coming, yet who knows how the gods reckon the passage of time? It is assuredly the same period of cleansing of this world that is prophesied in the final book of the Christians, but the prophet John did not possess the key to its understanding, and did not divine its true intention.

Those said to be marked by the Beast are those who bear the mark of Nyarlathotep, but the mark is concealed, not exposed to the uninitiated. Those marked by the Beast serve Nyarlathotep. The one hundred and forty-four thousand virgins spoken of by John are those of the living and of the dead who have pledged themselves before the black throne to Azathoth as his personal vassals, or who will pledge themselves in the future, to serve him forever when he regains his sight and his reason on the high seat, and restores the summer land. They are called virgins in the Revelation of John, from the purity of their transformed minds and bodies that remain after their elevation through the higher gates of Yog-Sothoth, which burn away in the flames of stars all their dross nature. As for the rest of unheeding humanity, when they die they become the wailing voices of despair in the black vortex that swirls around the chaos mount.

All that is written in the *Necronomicon* beneath the black throne shall come to pass, but only when it is read. What is written on unread pages of the book remains unfixed, and may be altered by time. The fate of every living creature in the cosmos is written therein, and those who are brought before the throne by Nyarlathotep to sign their names in blood in the book may read their own fates, if they dare to turn its pages. They have but one chance to read the *Necronomicon*—when they stand before the throne in their astral shells, where the book floats upon the air, awaiting their names, they have the power to turn its pages.

What they read in the *Necronomicon*, they remember only in dreams, for the mind mercifully blots out during waking life the knowledge of what is to come. Those who chance to remember the words of the book outside of their dreams at once run mad, though a few of them retain enough reason to write down some of what they have glimpsed before the black throne. One such madman was the poet of Yemen, Abdul Alhazred, who recorded some of what he read and remembered from his dreams, before the Old Ones sent their invisible servant to rend his flesh and lift him up to a higher sphere.

In imitation of the great book of all books, those who worship and serve the Old Ones in this world should make lesser books in which they record the laws of the Old Ones that apply to their own lives, and the progress of their work in magic. They shall put into their books the rituals they create for their own uses, and the communications and teachings they receive from the Old Ones and their servants, for each receives instruction according to his capacity. In memory of the black book beneath the black throne, they shall call their books the *Necronomicon*. The book will be different for each member of the Order of the Old Ones, yet always shall serve the same purpose—to train its maker in the arts of the occult, and to prepare his mind for the coming great work.

This preparation takes innumerable paths, for each man and woman serves the Old Ones in a different way, hardening the mind and heart against horrors that would drive the uninitiated mad in moments. Nyarlathotep will assign tasks to members of our Order each according to their abilities and circumstances in life. His words come into the ear like the buzzings of insects on the night breeze, and those who hear must heed. He tells them what they must do to prepare themselves to stand before the black throne, and how to inscribe their names in the *Necronomicon*. In the period before this attainment, they learn and work and serve, and he and the other lords favor true worship and offerings with worldly gifts.

No man may know when the final outcome prophesied in the pages of the black book will be fulfilled, for the number of its pages changes from moment to moment with each worldly event. The Work of the Trapezohedron may come to its fulfillment tomorrow, or not for a thousand years. Those who serve the Old Ones add their souls to the book when they die, increasing its power by tiny increments. The greater its power grows, the more tangibly the things written on its pages show themselves in the lower chaos, where we dwell among the damned.

The Three Ranks

Three ranks mark the levels of attainment among members of the Order of the Old Ones—Servant, Master, and Lord. All disciples who follow one of the seven ways pass through these grades, but not all attain the third and highest. Those who withdraw in fear before they reach the third level reject the Order, but they cannot reject the Old Ones, since they remain bound to them by their initial oath of obedience for the remainder of their lives, and at death their souls are taken, as are the souls of all others. They are not entered into the pages of the black book beneath the throne of chaos, for that honor belongs only to those who have attained enlightenment by means of one of the seven paths. No, they dance and whirl like dried husks in the wind around the chaos seat, becoming part of the dark maelstrom, and are lost in it.

A petitioner to join the Order of the Old Ones becomes a Servant of the Order when he accepts the mark of the Old Ones, and recites the oath of obedience. To be a Servant of the Order is to carry out the commands given by the Masters of the Order. These commands concern the maintenance of the Order, the fulfillment of the works of the Old Ones upon the earth, and the study of ritual magic, which is the main duty of all Servants.

No Master or Lord shall abuse his power by demeaning Servants of the Order, or by commanding them to perform unsuitable works. All members of the Order serve the Old Ones, whatever their rank. As they hope for favor and aid from their higher masters beyond the gates of Yog-Sothoth, so should they give favor and aid to those of lower rank who stand in need. Any Master who abuses a Servant is to be cast out and cursed. Any Lord who abuses a Master or a Servant is to be cast out and cursed.

Servants conduct themselves at all times with utmost humility toward their brothers and sisters in chaos, aware that their rank is the lowest of the low, and that they have no station of authority within the Order. Yet toward those outside the ranks of the Order they conduct themselves as lords, for so much higher are they in attainment than even the wisest and most powerful man or woman who has not taken the oath of obedience to the Old Ones. They do not boast, or threaten, but bear themselves with dignity, and when a demand is made that they speak about forbidden secrets, they respond with silence. The wishes and wants of the uninitiated are like the barkings of dogs, unheeded by the wise.

Where formal temples of the Order are maintained, it will be the duty of Servants to clean and repair them. It is also their task to guard these temples and ensure that they are not violated by the uninitiated, and to watch over them to prevent thefts and vandalism. Servants must study within the temples, where temples are available. Masters shall guide them in their studies. In those regions where no temples have been established, Servants may receive instruction at the homes of Masters, or where required by necessary in parks, plazas, or other private or public spaces in such corners and at such times when conversations will not be overheard.

The office of Servant is to carry out the more mundane works of the Old Ones. Servants perform whatever tasks are necessary to service the temple, or to aid the work of Masters or Lords. Servants share in the conduct of the cycle of weekly rites to the seven lords of the Old Ones when these rites are worked within temples or in stone circles beneath the stars where members of the Order gather. They shall receive higher instruction from Masters concerning communications with the Old Ones that are psychically sent, or given in dreams.

In this way, Servants began to form the personal ties of communication with the lords of the Old Ones and their lesser familiar creatures that will support their higher work in the Order. Through meditation and astral projection they seek the conversation and instruction of the Old Ones. They determine which of the seven paths they shall walk to the throne of chaos, whether through one of the four outer gates or one of the three inner gates, and begin their preliminary training for the future quest.

Servants may petition to be elevated to the rank of Master after the elapse of one full year following the date on which they assumed the rank of Servant. They shall be examined on the equinox that follows most closely the date of their petition by a Master who has held that rank for at least one full year, if such is available, and if they demonstrate by their responses that they understand the astral workings of the rites, the fundamentals of general ceremonial magic, and have attained the ability to project their awareness on the astral plane and to perceive astral events, the Master may grant them the second rank. Servants who fail the first examination may petition for testing on the next equinox, and so on until their knowledge and practical skills have been deemed acceptable, and the second rank granted.

A solitary practitioner who wishes to adore and work the rites of the Old Ones, having no Master to judge his fitness, shall assume the lowest rank of Servant and shall study with diligence and daily practice the rites for a full year. If he then believes himself fit for elevation to the second rank, on the equinox following the completion of a year of study, he may to be tested by the lord he has chosen for his mentor on the path to the black throne. This should be done ritually, within the stone circle, on the astral level. Absolute honesty is required, for if the higher lord denies the request, the judgment of the lord should be accepted until the next equinox.

A solitary magician who joins a temple of the Order of the Old Ones, and who has at some previous date advanced himself in rank to the rank of Master, must be tested by the Master or Masters of that temple, and must accept their judgment regarding his fitness to hold his self-adopted rank. If they so order it, he shall be demoted back to the rank of Servant for further instruction, and tested on the next equinox.

The mundane duties of those who hold the rank of Master involve executive decisions regarding the establishment or removal of Order temples, the acceptance of petitioners into the lowest rank of Servant within the temple, the disciplining of Order members both by overt and occult means, the casting out and cursing of members who have wantonly violated their oaths and obligations, and the composition of instruction guides for aiding the studies of Servants. Masters shall also compose and conduct unique rituals of magic for the attainment of desired purposes that forward the work of the Old Ones or benefit the lives of members of the Order and their agents.

The esoteric duties of Masters involve sustaining links of communication with the lords of the Old Ones, for the purpose of receiving occult wisdom in dreams and through psychic channels, and maintaining the continuing prosperity and good fortune of the Order, as well as engaging in the quest for personal attainment that leads by one of the four outer or three inner ways to the ninety-three steps of the throne of chaos, where their names are entered in their own blood on the pages of the *Necronomicon*.

When receiving communications from the Old Ones, they may be assisted by Servants who have demonstrated uncommon aptitude as psychics—for know that passive psychic perception is innate and does not need to be studied, although study and practice will strengthen it and render it more reliable. Some members of the Order will, by their natures, be more open to communications from the Old Ones, even though they be of the rank of Servant, and wise Masters will understand when and how to make use of their gifts.

In their personal quest to stand before the black throne, there is none who may aid the Masters, since the needed transformations in body and mind can only be accomplished by the individual who walks along the way—they cannot be conferred by other Masters, no matter how long their seniority or what their level of attainment, no, not even by Lords. There is no set period for this quest, which may require one year or twenty years. Only when a Master succeeds in opening the gate of Yog-Sothoth on his chosen path will Nyarlathotep consent to become his guide, and only when the Crawling Chaos has revealed the way will the Master be enabled to walk the path, which is fraught with difficulty and peril, to the very steps of the black throne. This is a process of becoming that may require years of dedicated ritual work.

Those who succeed in reaching the black throne on the astral level shall sign their names in blood in the *Necronomicon* and receive a private mark on some part of their body from Nyarlathotep, as a token of their obedience to him and to the Work of the Trapezohedron. Or, they may choose to receive the mark of Azathoth in place of the mark of Nyarlathotep—this is a matter of personal choice and no coercion may be used to influence the choice. After returning in awareness to their physical bodies, they will find this mark, usually in some hidden place, when they search for it. This elevates them to the rank of Lord, for as the lords of the Old Ones rule the higher spheres through the gates of Yog-Sothoth, so do the Lords of the Order rule this lower sphere of men and beasts. Good fortune is theirs by virtue of the favor of the Old Ones, and they have the power to grant fortune to others or to withdraw it from those who have displeased them.

The Lords of the Order shall maintain lines of communication with each other, no matter where they dwell or have their circles. In division is weakness, but in union is strength. All serve the Old Ones, regardless of rank or nation. There shall be no factional disorder between temples or leaders, but all division must be resolved by reasoned discussion. There is but one *Necronomicon* of which all others are mere copies, one stone circle of the art in many places, one gate of Yog-Sothoth that opens on many worlds, and one throne of chaos to unite all discords.

The Seven Ways

The seven ways to the attainment of the throne of chaos are not to be found on any map, but are represented thematically by the seven directions of space that surround the stone circle, and by the lords of the Old Ones associated with those directions. Four of the ways are linked with the outer lords and are not beyond the capacity of most devoted practitioners, but three of the ways are tied to the inner lords and require the utmost dedication. Of those three, the way of the center, which is the path of Azathoth, is the most daunting. As a consequence, most disciples are advised to attempt one of the outer gates that are marked by the threshold rods beyond the stone circle. Let it be understood that no path is more worthy than the other six, for all lead to the same destination, the throne of chaos.

It is the primary work of self-perfection for Masters of the Order to walk their chosen ways until they attain the black throne. Only by daily devotion to his path of attainment shall a Master be enabled to open the gate of Yog-Sothoth upon that way, and obtain the guidance of Nyarlathotep, the soul and messenger of the dancing gods. Only when guided by the Crawling Chaos shall a Master attain to the lowest of the ninety-three steps at the base of the chaos mount and climb them to the black throne.

The north gate is the way of Yig. It involves physical austerities and self-sacrifice, and the disciplining of the body through sustained postures and controlled breathing. Masters who follow this path will control their diet and will harden their bodies with daily exercise. They will cultivate self-discipline through denial of their impulses and passions. Trials of physical endurance that expose the body to hardship and fatigue will open the north gate. Masters who walk this path must take care not to damage the vehicle of their flesh through an excess of zeal. They make Yig their patron lord, and call upon this lord of the Old One for strength to endure, and for guidance in their austerities.

The east gate is the way of Shub-Niggurath. It relies on heightened sexual energies to awaken psychic and magic abilities. Masters who walk this path submerge themselves in pleasurable sensations, and indulge in various forms of sexual excess, in order to achieve the maximum arousal of sexual energy from its sleeping place at the base of the spine. They make the obscene goddess Shub-Niggurath their patroness and invoke her unceasingly into their lives, and into their beds. She comes to them in dreams and lies with them, and whispers the secrets they require to open the east gate. Masters who worship Shub-Niggurath as the key to the gate must have a care to avoid becoming so lost in pleasure that they forget their higher purpose.

The south gate is the way of Cthulhu. It requires intense training of the will, until it is made into a sharp weapon that can thrust through all obstacles and dominate all opponents. Masters who tread the path of Cthulhu use martial exercises of the body and mind to increase determination, training in combat with the knife, the sword, the staff, and the gun, as well as with the bare hands. They practice concentration and visualization, until they can hold their intention unwaveringly for hours on any object or idea, and can conceive images in their minds with all the clarity of normal vision. They may acquire the ability to project their thoughts into the minds of others, and even to direct the actions of others with thought alone, just as mighty Cthulhu once commanded his worshippers from his house on R'lyeh with thought alone. They are able to pierce veils of deception and illusion, to see deeply into the hearts of other men. Their potent will gives them command over lesser beings.

The west gate is the way of Dagon. It is the path of the intellectual study of arcane knowledge. Masters who tread this path become scholars of all forms of the occult arts, and seek learning from ancient books and revered teachers both in this material sphere and on higher astral spheres. Their study includes the making of sigils, the vibration of words of power, various forms of divination, the use of gates and portals, and also the summoning and commanding of spirits. They make themselves wise in the lore of the higher realms and their inhabitants. They call upon Dagon, who is as old as time and great in wisdom, as their patron lord, and request that he instruct them in the subjects they must study in order to acquire the degree of attainment that will win the approval of Nyarlathotep, for only the *chaos that crawls* can guide the way to the black throne.

These are the four outer gates: the north gate of Yig is the way of physical discipline and austerities, the east gate of Shub-Niggurath the way of sensual indulgence, the south gate of Cthulhu the way of willful dominance, and the west gate of Dagon the way of deep scholarship. All gates are different in appearance, yet all open on dark and perilous roads that end at the black throne of Azathoth at the vortex of ultimate chaos. It is difficult to walk these roads, and impossible to avoid wandering into the wilderness without a guide. Only Nyarlathotep can show the way. Open the gate through your devotion to the path you have chosen, and the Crawling Chaos will await you on the other side. Obey his instructions, and he will lead you to the black throne.

Approach to the throne may also be had through the three inner gates of the higher lords, but these ways are more difficult and fraught with dangers that cannot be predicted. The inner gates are so termed because they are marked by the altar rods at the center of the stone circle, and are associated with the vertical axis of space.

The upper gate of Yog-Sothoth is opened by the perfection of the art of astral travel and familiarity with the spiritual creatures that dwell on the astral planes, each of which is a separate world with its own landscape and inhabitants. The blue rod of the altar marks its way of approach. Projection of the astral shell is of necessity the study of the disciples of all seven gates, but those who place themselves under the guidance of Yog-Sothoth seek to excel in it and to master its use. This first of the inner ways differs from the four outer ways in not employing an external training or discipline—for the way of Yig concerns perfection of the body, the way of Shub-Niggurath the exploration of sensations, the way of Cthulhu mastery of combat and the will, and the way of Dagon the study of texts and other outwardly recorded teachings.

The lower gate of Nyarlathotep is passed by dedication to dark works of necromancy, and close communication with the shades of the dead. The orange rod of the altar marks it. By the creatures and trappings of death is the disciple exalted and perfected. He makes as his study all dead things, and all trappings associated with death and the tomb, and acquires wisdom from the shades who flock to his circle. To follow the way of this inner gate is a perilous undertaking for the disciple, who suffers a threefold return in consequence for any outrage he may commit against the sanctity of the dead, either knowingly or by chance. Nyarlathotep will guide him in learning the skills of necromancy, but will not protect him from the consequences. Only those with a natural affinity for death should choose this approach to the black throne.

The central gate of Azathoth is opened by means of meditation on nothingness. Although it is marked by the yellow rod of the altar, no transition along a path is necessary in order to pass through this inner gate, since it resides at the center of the self. Those who choose to follow this path return to where they began, and discover the black throne by seeking within their own mind and heart. Yet it is necessary to venture far through tangled wildernesses of confusion and doubt before the end of the quest is attained. Meditation is done in a seated posture. The mind is made as empty as that of Azathoth, and the eyes are closed to simulate the blindness of the lord of chaos. Music and chants may be used as an aid in meditation, but in the end there is only silence.

When at last you stand at the lowermost step of the throne mount, the heavens of chaos filled with the darkly glittering vortex of lost souls that forever mingle their howls of despair with the uncertain music of Azathoth's cracked flute, you must climb the steps without assistance. Then will your months or years of training on the quest be tested, for each of the ninety-three stairs on the hell mount is a test. Nyarlathotep will watch in amusement but will not intervene. If you falter, your soul will be ripped away from your astral body on the whirling wind and lost before it can be dedicated to the Work of the Trapezohedron.

If you reach the throne, Nyarlathotep will remove the *Necronomicon* from its shadowed space beneath the black seat and set it open upon the very air itself. You will be given the chance to turn its pages, if you dare. Then the Crawling Chaos will cut your astral body so that you bleed, giving you a mark that you will wear for the remainder of your earthly life, and beyond, for the mark made in the astral shell shows itself upon the living flesh. From this blood you must sign your name in the book of the laws of the dead, and must pledge yourself body and soul to the Old Ones and their higher purposes.

Nyarlathotep will ask you to swear fealty to him, but if you are wise and if you remember yourself—for all this is like a dream and bewilders the mind when it is attained—you will instead swear your service to Azathoth, the blind lord of chaos. Nyarlathotep will gnash his teeth, but this is lawful and he cannot punish you for this devotion to Azathoth, since he himself is bound in service to the idiot god. If instead, you choose to bind yourself to Nyarlathotep, he will reward you in this life, but may exact payment for his gifts in tasks that are not part of the great work, but serve his selfish purposes. If you swear loyalty to Nyarlathotep, the mark he gave you is his mark; but if you swear loyalty to Azathoth, the mark is the mark of the blind god, impressed in your flesh by his messenger.

By this act of dedication and this oath, you become a Lord of the Order of the Old Ones upon this earth, sworn to serve the Old Ones in all things that tend to the fulfillment of the Work of the Trapezohedron, which is the purification of this globe and her elevation through the highest gate of Yog-Sothoth to the chaos mount, where, cleansed of her heavy clay, Barbelzoa shall resume her rightful place on the left-hand seat of the triple throne. By this oath you make yourself a foe to all men who have not devoted themselves to the Old Ones, and to all races abiding on this sphere, both alien and native, who have not acquired in their nature by devotion and works a part of the likeness of the Old Ones.

So have many Christians sworn in their ignorance, for they embrace the prophecies of John as written in his Revelations, which predict the coming end time of great destruction, and the exaltation among the stars of the Queen of Heaven from her lowly whoredom among the beasts. They celebrate the great work, but know not what they anticipate with such eagerness. They are chaff for the flames. Only the Lords of the Order, in direct communication with the lords of the Old Ones themselves, may understand the true meaning of the end times predicted by John, when the four gates at the watchtowers of this world swing wide, and the hosts that serve the Old Ones rush in to burn and destroy and lay waste to the lands and seas.

Then shall the lord Nyarlathotep wield his fiery sword, separating the few who are chosen from the many who are damned. The favored few who bear the marks shall receive new bodies of the same alien flesh as the bodies of the Old Ones themselves, having prepared their minds to receive them, but the many who are damned shall become as bits of ash rising in the blast of a furnace. He will strip away the sea and rock of this world with his sword and seize the naked goddess, carrying her upward on his dragon wings through the spheres that have no names, and his servants shall follow in his wake.

Should his will to power remain unopposed by watchful Yog-Sothoth, a new aeon will commence, and Nyarlathotep will rule the cosmos, emboldened by his matings with Barbelzoa even at the very feet of her blind father, who in his idiocy will know nothing of the outrage. He will impose order on the many worlds, but it will be an order of his own design, a dark order of repression and constraint. All this is prophesied to come to pass, yet it may come tomorrow, or it may not come in the lifetimes of many men. In the meanwhile, those who serve the Old Ones reap advantages in this world and during this term of existence. It is better to serve in this world than to burn in the next.

BOOK OF THE SOUTH GATE:
PRACTICE

The Order of the Old Ones

The Order of the Old Ones shall be established for the study of the Old Ones, their history, nature, and works, and for interaction with them by means of regular rites, special rituals, offerings, sacrifices, prayers, observances, and psychic communion. It is open to both men and women of eighteen years or older. Candidates seeking admission to the Order must acknowledge the Old Ones as the secret rulers of this world, and agree to advance their purposes and aid in the consummation of the Work of the Trapezohedron, which is the purification of this fallen earth, and her eventual restoration to her original spiritual estate on the left-hand seat of the triple throne of chaos.

Petitioners admitted to the Order must take an oath of obedience, in which they swear to remain faithful to the teachings of the Old Ones, as they are transmitted to leaders of the Order, to serve them without hesitation, and to hold the teachings and works of the order secret. Violation of the oath shall result in expulsion from the Order and the curse of Nyarlathotep upon the head of the violator.

New members serve not less than one year in the rank of Servant, learning the outward working of the daily rites of the seven lords and studying the teachings of the Order. Servants perform the physical labors required to maintain the temples of the Order, and must obey the instructions of members of higher rank, except those instructions that are a danger to their well-being, or an insult to their honor.

After examination upon the equinox following the completion of the year-long term, and elevation to the rank of Master, members supervise and manage the running of the affairs of the Order, and preside over the daily and semi-annual rites, as well as any special ritual workings that arise by petition of members, or out of necessity. The rank of Master has no set term. The primary responsibility of Masters is to walk one of the seven ways of attainment to the throne of chaos, there to enter their names into the *Necronomicon* and receive the mark of Nyarlathotep, or the mark of Azathoth, upon their bodies.

Those bearing either of these marks, which are given by Nyarlathotep before the black throne, achieve the rank of Lords of the Order. It is part of their function to make decisions regarding changes of routine, write teaching texts, receive direct communications and instructions from the Old Ones and their agents, and sit in judgment over disputes that arise among members. Theirs is the power to establish and dissolve temples of the Order, as changing circumstances require. Lords cannot be judged, except by those of their own rank, or by the Old Ones themselves. A Lord guilty of dishonorable acts, or acts that injure the well-being of the Order, may be expelled from the order by a judgment of three other Lords, rendered in writing.

Temples of the Old Ones shall be established in septemvirs and their multiples. A minimum of seven members who have among them a Master shall be sufficient to establish a new temple. A temple may affiliate itself with an existing school of the Order, provided approval in writing can be gained from a Lord of that school. A school consists of an association of temples of like-minded members who perform the same works, and follow the directives of a single elected leader. The leader of a school of the Order shall be a Lord duly elected by secret ballot at a gathering of Lords and Masters of the associated temples. Lords may establish new temples. A Lord who authorizes a new temple becomes karmically responsible for its works, so such authorization should not be given lightly.

Temples are established under the benevolent authority of one of the seven lords of the Old Ones, who becomes the patron lord of that temple. A temple under the benevolence of Dagon becomes the Dagon Temple of the Old Ones; a temple under the benevolence of Yig becomes the Yig Temple. Individual temples are distinguished by their locations. A temple under the benevolence of Cthulhu that is located in Chicago would be called the Cthulhu Chicago Temple.

Any existing temple in a community that bears the title of a lord of the Old Ones has prior claim on the patronage of that lord, and no newly established temple in the same community shall adopt the same lord, unless all seven of the lords have been adopted by seven temples. A temple may then take the name of a lord a second time in the same city, but must distinguish itself by its local place name—its political riding, borough, local community, or even by its street name. In this way, all temples shall be uniquely named, and confusion avoided.

As many as seven members may serve inside the stone circle to conduct the rites. Large temples must rotate their members so that all have the opportunity to conduct the rites, and learn their correct manner of observance. The other members shall gather around the circle and observe the rites, although attendance on all daily rites is not a requirement for those outside the circle. Those most senior may sit between the stones, becoming part of the circle itself. Additional members of the temple shall sit outside the circle, beyond the thresholds of the four gates, where there is sufficient space to accommodate them.

The members of a temple may move to a new building with the approval of all its Masters, when circumstances dictate. Such a move does not constitute the establishment of a new temple. If the membership of a temple grows too large for its effective working of the rites, the Masters of the temple may petition a Lord to establish a new temple in addition to the old temple, in this way multiplying the places of worship for the Order.

The teachings of the Order are passed down from mentor to student. Each Master shall have Servants as students, and shall instruct them personally in a private setting, and periodically question them to test their knowledge. Masters shall instruct Servants, and Lords shall instruct Masters. In circumstances where there are gaps in the ranks of the Order, any member of higher rank may instruct any member of lower rank in the knowledge required for the lower rank. Those of the same rank may gather for study and debate on questions of practical magic.

In recognition that there will always exist isolated individuals or small groups who wish to become members of the Order of the Old Ones but lack access to an established temple, self-initiation shall be acknowledged as legitimate. The self-initiated Servant of the order must take the oath of initiation before the lords of the Old Ones in the stone circle, and must study and practice the daily rites for a full year before, on the following equinox, presuming to elevate himself to the rank of Master.

Self-initiated Servants and Masters who seek to join an established temple shall suffer examination by the Masters or Lord of the temple, who may deny admission if they believe the candidate unfit, or if they judge that the assumption of the rank of Master has been premature. At their discretion, they may demote a self-initiated Master to the rank of Servant for further training, and admit him to the temple in that lower rank.

Groups of self-initiated Servants may form their own temple, if they have among them at least one Master, and if their number is at least seven. No temple shall be established with fewer than seven members. Should such a self-formed temple seek to join an established school, it must suffer to have itself examined before the Lords of that school, who will judge its fitness to join the school.

Work of the Trapezohedron

The Work of the Trapezohedron is the great labor of the Old Ones to return the fallen and sleeping goddess Barbelzoa to her original place at the left hand of Azathoth on the throne of chaos. All of their lesser labors on this world tend to this single higher purpose. It was for this reason that they came through the gates of Yog-Sothoth and assumed the semblances of material forms. Nyarlathotep directs the work in his own way and for his own reasons, but he is not Lord of Chaos. That title belongs to the god whose true name is never spoken, he who squats upon the blackened throne and unreels the ages with his music.

It is called the Work of the Trapezohedron because the higher dimensional geometry of the final gate of Yog-Sothoth, through which the goddess must be raised, has a shape that resembles in our reality that of a trapezohedron with eleven sides. When the gate is opened, Yog-Sothoth unfolds the sides from their hidden dimensions like the petals of a flower from its bud. Past the gate exists the ultimate reality, which is perceived in forms that are limited by the mind of the perceiver—for know you that all the forms of the Old Ones are no more than masks.

There are two parts to this great work. The first necessitates the cleansing of the surface of this globe, which is the solidified body of the sleeping goddess, from all forms of lower life that have been carried here across space, or that evolved here in its primal beginnings. This is usually understood in a mundane sense, as a slaughter of life, but will be effected not by killing, by through transformation. The lower will become higher, the material will be made spiritual. When the stars are right and the Old Ones return, they will begin this cleansing, and their chosen instruments will take part in the labor with great joy and exultation. The Old Ones will empower their servants so that even the least of their Order strides the earth like a god, casting lightning and fire.

The second part of the labor is the opening of the successive gates of Yog-Sothoth, which are in truth merely levels of a single gate. Each level must be passed before the next may be opened. As this globe makes transition through each level, she shall become less substantial, more ethereal, until all the dross matter has faded away and only the brightly shining soul of the goddess remains naked at the center. The lower substance will not vanish into nothingness but will be transformed by its translation through the gates. When the shining trapezohedron is opened, the earth will vanish from her orbit about the sun.

The second part of the labor, the elevation through the gates, cannot commence until the first part has been completed, the purification of all life. The first part has been hindered for aeons by the poisonous alignment of the stars and planets, which conspire in their winding courses across the heavens to cast down a combination of rays noxious to the substance of the Old Ones. Cthulhu, the great war-priest of the Old Ones who dreams beneath the waves of the Pacific Ocean, has prophesied that in the fullness of time, the stars will come right once again, but not even he with his alien science can predict when that time will be, for the complexity of the calculation defeats him. It is said that the Yithians, who are wisest of all beings in the cosmos, knew the date, but if so they did not choose to reveal it to the lesser races before they vanished into the distant future.

In the meanwhile, the Old Ones work their preparations through their mortal and immortal agents dwelling both on this sphere and in higher spheres, who are not troubled by the poison of the stars and can travel through the gates with impunity. The Old Ones seek to breed with human women and engender hybrid offspring in their wombs, to advance the great work. They are ever watchful for receptive wombs for their seed, and agents that will nurture its growth in secret until the growths are strong enough to care for themselves. Yet they are cautious, and do not seek to breed more than a few at a time, having learned from their error. In times past they bred too many, and their children rebelled from their authority and sought to conquer the world for their own use. For their hubris the Old Ones were forced to destroy them, by the instrument of a great flood.

The ritual work of preparing a womb for impregnation by an Old One may be referred to as the Work of the Trapezohedron within the ranks of the Order, since it is the lower reflection on the level of humanity of the great work of restoration, just as a Lord of the Order is a lower reflection of a lord of the Old Ones. By mingling our blood with the seed of the Old Ones, the flesh of our race is made ethereal, and fit to pass upward through the gates of Yog-Sothoth. At the same time our transmuted flesh shields the essence of the Old Ones from the malign rays of the stars, as the shell of a lobster protects the tenderness within, so that the minds of the Old Ones can function in this world, using the hybrids for their hands.

In the past, some of these hybrids have been monsters. It is true that they may range the full spectrum between the nature and appearance of the Old Ones themselves, and the nature and appearance of a normal human being. The lords have learned wisdom, for in the past the monsters who differed greatly from the human form were invariably destroyed, either by their own chaotic actions, or by human beings who reviled them for their differences. In more recent times the Old Ones only breed hybrids who will be born with the semblance of true humanity, so that they may pass in our world unnoticed and unhindered by others of this lower race.

A scattering of agents with mixed blood roam the world and fulfill their appointed tasks, obedient to the inner whisperings of the Old Ones, who talk to them in their dreams. They have a natural affinity for the lore of the Old Ones, and for the practice of ceremonial magic. They do not know their own true natures, but believe themselves afflicted by a kind of madness that they carefully conceal from others. The purposes of the Old Ones are veiled and complex, and are not apparent in their individual works. These agents of mixed blood commit acts that to the uninitiated may appear to be meaningless, yet their higher meaning works its effect unseen beneath the surface of reality, as slowly the web of the Old Ones is woven across the face of the world.

Those who serve the Old Ones are never asked to perform acts that will result in their own destruction, for the lords of the Old Ones value their human agents. At times the purpose of their commands may not be apparent, and the acts may seem to accomplish nothing of use. Their purpose is hidden from our level of consciousness but open on higher levels. Acts of obedience rightly fulfilled are rewarded. The Old Ones will care for the members of the Order who commit their lives to the great work.

Oath of Obedience

This oath shall be administered to all who seek entrance to the Order of the Old Ones at the lowest rank of Servant. It must be freely voiced by the candidate for admission, and witnessed by a Master or a Lord, unless it is voiced during a self-initiation, in which circumstance the lords of the Old Ones will bear witness. The oath is presented to the candidate in printed form, and the candidate reads it aloud, and then inscribes his signature at the bottom in acknowledgement of understanding and acceptance. The inscribed document is to be retained by the Masters of the temple. Should at some future time the admitted candidate violate his oath, his signature may be occultly employed as an instrument of punishment, if this is deemed necessary by the presiding Lord of the temple.

Of my free will I enter the ranks of the Order of the Old Ones, and pledge my obedience and service to the Old Ones and all their works, including the Work of the Trapezohedron. I swear to uphold the laws of the Order, and to diligently devote myself to the study of its teachings and rites. I further swear to keep all its wisdom and works secret from the uninitiated, to protect and aid all brothers and sisters of the Order in times of need, and to obey the directives of those brothers and sisters who are senior to me in rank or in term of membership, provided the fulfillment of those directives is in no way injurious to myself.

I commit myself to the personal discipline of the Seven Ways of Chaos, that by open-ing the gate of Yog-Sothoth upon my chosen path among the seven, I may stand before the black throne of Azathoth and inscribe my name in the Necronomicon beside the names of the Lords of the Order. Freely and of my own will I acknowledge and declare the Old Ones to be the rightful stewards of this world and all it contains, and myself their humble and obedient agent.

Should I betray the terms of this oath, let me be thrust forth from this Order, and let all brothers and sisters turn their backs on me. Let Nyarlathotep send down his wrath upon my head and darken my life with misfortune. Let me never know peace or happiness even to the moment of my death, but let me be hounded by the grinning black dogs of Tindalos, and let my soul be whirled up like a dry leaf upon the vortex of chaos to swirl around the black throne, howling its anguish for eternity.

Voiced and inscribed by me before a superior of the Order of the Old Ones this _____ day of the month _____ in the common year _____.

_____

(your signature)

Nightly Obeisance

The nightly Obeisance is to be recited each night before retiring to bed to sleep, while standing and facing the north. With feet together and back straight, raise your hands and place the tips of your fingers across your closed eyelids in imitation of the blindness of the dancing gods, who see with higher vision. Intone the declaration while visualizing the fivefold mark of the Old Ones floating upon your inner darkness behind your forehead. If necessary to conceal the words from being overheard, they may be whispered or delivered *sub voce*.

> The Old Ones were, the Old Ones are, the Old Ones shall be. Unseen by men, you walk beneath the moon and stars. Where you tread, the corn is beaten into the field and trees are torn from their roots. Your passing is like the roar of a great storm, and behind you lingers the odor of thunder.

> Accept me as your human agent! Freely I offer my mind and body for your use. Make of me your instrument in the Work of the Trapezohedron, that the earth shall be purified and restored to her rightful seat on the chaos mount!

May the seven lords guide me through the cycle of the week. May the twelve dancing gods favor all my works through the turning wheel of the year. Watch over and protect my life, that I may serve the black throne all of my days.

Let it be so!

Rite of Dagon
(Monday)

The seven daily rites corresponding to the days of the week should be conducted within the stone circle at a convenient hour that does not conflict with the mundane daily obligations of the worshipper. It is best to work them at the same hour of the day on all the days of the week. The daily ritual opens the day, and the nightly Obeisance closes the day.

Wear the sash of the lord for which the ritual is worked, and the lamen of that lord around your neck. Individual members of the Order who cannot go to the temple to observe their daily rituals, or who have no temple, should conduct them within their own personal stone circle.

Place the geometric key to the gate of Dagon, the crescent of the moon, in the center of the altar triangle alongside the white-wrapped Elder Seal, and light the three lights at the points of the altar. Written prayers asking Dagon to grant specific requests may be folded and placed within the altar. A material offering to Dagon may also be placed in the triangle by any participant in the ritual who seeks a special favor or dispensation from the god. Offerings of silver are appropriate for this lord, as are offerings of sea shells and crystals, which are watery by their occult nature. After the ritual, all offerings should be discarded and not used again for any purpose, since their astral essences have been given as gifts to the god.

Stand in the circle facing the altar on its blue, southern side, so that you look across it toward the north. This is the beginning posture for all rituals. Speak these opening words:

On this day of Dagon, I invoke the Lord of the Seas.

Remove the key of Dagon from the altar, and walk around the altar counterclockwise to stand facing the purple stone of Dagon with the altar triangle behind you. Bend and strike the stone of Dagon with the key in your right hand, holding it lightly between your fingers so that it vibrates freely and produces a clear tone, then walk around the altar in a counterclockwise direction, striking the other stones as you pass them with the key.

In this way a chaotic circle of Dagon is established on the astral level—chaotic because it is traced in a direction opposite that of the course of the sun across the heavens. This counterclockwise direction of movement is known as widdershins. All movement around the circle is widdershins. As you return to the purple stone of Dagon, strike it gently a second time with the key to seal the circle by joining its end with its beginning. Speak the words:

The circle is joined!

Any other members of the Order who share the ritual circle with you should space themselves at equal intervals around the altar at the beginning of the rite, and should walk around the altar as you walk to project the circle, keeping the same distance from you so that all in the circle complete a full circumambulation and return to their starting places. A maximum of six others may share the ritual with you, if the circle is large enough to accommodate them, but others may sit between the stones, or if necessary may sit beyond the outer gates to observe. All who observe are participants in the ritual, and lend their energies to its fulfillment.

Standing once again before the purple stone of Dagon, visualize on the astral level rays of purple light connecting the seven stones, so that they form a heptagon of light. The stones may be visualized as larger in the astral world than they are in the physical world, so that they stand up to the level of your heart, and the purple band of light that connects them floats in the air at heart level.

Walk around the circle widdershins until you stand in the west. Hold the key of Dagon by its end, pointing it with your right arm extended through the circle at the Gate of the West, which is located above the purple threshold rod on the western side of the circle. Recite the following litany of Dagon:

> Great Dagon, dweller in ocean rifts, mate of Hydra whose womb is forever fertile, lord of the Deep Ones who are your children under the waves, sovereign over all that dwell within the seas and waterways of the world, you who have been called Leviathan and Kraken and Cetus, approach this stone circle through the Gate of the West.
>
> Receive this offering as a tribute of respect and fidelity. Confer good fortune on all who stand within this circle, and all who observe this rite. Heed the prayers of those who have placed offerings upon the altar. Bless the works of the Order of the Old Ones that are done in your name, and in the names of the seven lords. Send your agents to watch over and protect all who serve you this day, and all the days of their lives.
>
> Yiii-eeee, Dagon! Lord of the Deep!

Press the key of Dagon to your forehead, kiss the key, then hold it close to your chest over your heart beneath your folded hands, and, with eyes closed, will the purple ray of Dagon to shine through the opened Gate of the West above the western threshold rod. Visualize the gate opening on the astral level and the light of Dagon shining through your body and into the circle to concentrate itself above the altar triangle.

After a minute or two of silent meditation, during which you should hold Dagon within your heart and contemplate his greatness, open your eyes and circumambulate widdershins to stand before the stone of Dagon. Strike the key of Dagon gently against his stone. Speak the words:

> The circle is broken!

Visualize on the astral level the heptagon of light connecting the stones break at the stone of Dagon and vanish. Walk around the circle widdershins to stand facing the blue rod at the base of the altar, and replace the key of Dagon within the altar. Bow your head in silent meditation for a minute or so. Put out the altar lights and remove your lamen of Dagon and purple sash to formally end the ritual. Discard with care and dignity any written prayers or offerings to Dagon that are within the altar.

Rite of Cthulhu
(Tuesday)

The rite of Cthulhu, which is performed on the day of the week devoted to this god of war, follows the same general pattern as that of Dagon, and all the other day rituals to the seven lords. Those who perform his rite within the stone circle wear the lamen of Cthulhu around their necks and the red sash of the lord tied around their waists over their black ritual robes, or if they have no robes, over black clothing devoted to ritual use.

An offering to Cthulhu, along with any prayers for his intervention, is placed within the altar triangle. Appropriate offerings include small objects of iron and steel, magnets, onions and other spices that are hot and sharp on the tongue, knives, images of weapons, and in general anything with a fiery, willful, or martial association. Also within the triangle are placed the Elder Seal in its white protective covering, and the key of Cthulhu, which has the shape of a trapezoid.

As leader of the rite, or as sole practitioner if it is done without companions in the circle, you light the flames at the points of the altar and stand before the blue altar rod, facing northward across the altar. Speak the opening words:

On this day of Cthulhu, I invoke the Lord of War.

Remove the key of Cthulhu from the altar and circumambulate the altar widdershins to stand in front of the red stone of Cthulhu. Strike the stone with his key and walk around the circle of stones widdershins, bending to strike each stone as you pass with the key, so that it rings with its distinctive tone. Once again rap the key on the stone of Cthulhu to close and complete the circle. Any companions with you in the circle must walk as you walk, keeping the same separation from you at all times. Speak the words:

The circle is joined!

As you stand before the red stone of Cthulhu, visualize on the astral level rays of ruby light connecting all seven of the stones to form a heptagon of light. The astral stones may be imagined as larger than the physical stones, so that the heptagon of red light floats at the level of your heart.

Walk around the circle against the course of the sun to reach the south. All movement in the circle is counterclockwise—never walk in a clockwise direction around the circle, even for a short step, since clockwise circumambulation represents order, and the Old Ones are lords of chaos. Hold the key of Cthulhu by its corner and extend your right arm through the circle to point with the key toward the Gate of the South, which may be visualized on the astral level as a translucent rectangle that stands above the red threshold rod in the south. Recite the following litany of Cthulhu:

Mighty Cthulhu, ruler of sunken R'lyeh, high priest of the Old Ones, autogenitor of the warrior spawn like to you in form, who bore the race of K'n-yan across the black gulf on leathern wings, you who dream in death within your stone house at the base of the obelisk of uncouth angles, approach this stone circle through the Gate of the South.

Receive this offering as a tribute of respect and fidelity. Confer good fortune on all who stand within this circle, and all who observe this rite. Heed the prayers of those who have placed offerings upon the altar. Bless the works of the Order of the Old Ones that are done in your name, and in the names of the seven lords. Send your agents to watch over and protect all who serve you this day, and all the days of their lives.

Yiii-eeee, Cthulhu! Lord of Dreams!

Touch the trapezoid key of Cthulhu to your forehead between your eyebrows above the bridge of your nose, and kiss the key with reverence. Hold it against your chest over your heart beneath your folded hands. With your eyes shut, will the ruby ray of Cthulhu to shine through the center of the opened Gate of the South, and through your body, so that it fills the circle with radiance that concentrates itself in the air above the altar.

Meditate silently with eyes shut for a minute or two, during which you should consider the resolve and might of Cthulhu, whose will is indomitable, and whose incorruptible and self-renewing body will endure until the end of time. It is impossible for Cthulhu to actually attend upon the circle, since he lies imprisoned beneath the waves, but his awareness will be called across space through the opened gate.

Walk around the circle widdershins to stand before the red stone of Cthulhu. Strike it gently with the key of Cthulhu and speak the words:

The circle is broken!

Visualize the ruby rays that form the heptagon of red light break apart on either side of the stone, and vanish. Circumambulate the circle widdershins to stand in the south, facing the blue altar rod at the base of the altar triangle. Put the key of Cthulhu back into the altar. Bow your head and silently meditate for a minute or two to clear your thoughts and calm your emotions. Then extinguish the altar lights to formally end the ritual, remove your lamen and sash of Cthulhu, and discard with care any prayers or offerings to Cthulhu that may reside within the altar.

Rite of Nyarlathotep
(Wednesday)

The day rite of Nyarlathotep, who is one of the three greater lords, is performed in a slightly different way from the day rite of the four lesser lords. Because the threshold of the gate of this lord forms part of the altar, rather than being located beyond the stone circle, the litany is directed inward instead of outward. In other respects, the structure of the ritual is similar to that of the lesser lords.

Place any written prayers or material offerings to Nyarlathotep into the altar triangle. Nyarlathotep represents the dark abyss and the dead, so things that are black, poisonous, or sterile are appropriate offerings, such as black stones, thorns or nettles, dead stinging insects, or anything connected with death, such as black feathers, coffin nails, or bones, may be given as offerings. Nyarlathotep is a psychopomp, having some similarities with Hermes and Thoth. Also within the altar triangle are placed the key of Nyarlathotep and the Elder Seal, securely wrapped and tied in its white shroud.

Wearing the lamen and orange sash of Nyarlathotep, stand in the south and light the three lights of the altar. Speak the opening words:

On this day of Nyarlathotep, I invoke the Lord of Chaos.

Take up the key of Nyarlathotep in your right hand and walk widdershins around the altar to stand before the orange stone of this lord. Strike the stone with the key and walk completely around the circle against the course of the sun, striking each stone in the circle as you pass. Touch the key a second time to the orange stone when you complete the circumambulation in order to join the end of the circle with its beginning. Say the words:

The circle is joined!

Visualize on the astral level rays of orange light connecting all seven stones in the circle, so that they form a heptagon of light with the stones at its points. The color should be distinctly different from the ruby rays of Cthulhu, so that you never confuse them in your imagination.

Move around the circle in a widdershins direction until you stand before the orange rod that forms the left side of the altar triangle. This is the threshold to the Gate of the Depths, the direction of space that belongs to Nyarlathotep.

Holding the key of Nyarlathotep by its end so that its triangular point is directed outward, extend it across the orange threshold rod of the altar in a sharp downward direction, so that it points below the ground or floor on which the stone circle has been erected, beneath the center of the altar. Recite this litany of Nyarlathotep:

> *Crafty Nyarlathotep, soul of the Nameless One, messenger of the twelve dancing gods of creation, faceless wanderer who keeps the lesser gods of earth enthralled in Kadath, who leads true disciples of the Old Ones to the foot of the black throne, master of the Necronomicon, wise in the ways of death, you who are called the Crawling Chaos, approach this stone circle through the Gate of the Depths.*
>
> *Receive this offering as a tribute of respect and fidelity. Confer good fortune on all who stand within this circle and all who observe this rite. Heed the prayers of those who have placed offerings upon the altar. Bless the works of the Order of the Old Ones that are done in your name, and in the names of the seven lords. Send your agents to watch over and protect all who serve you this day, and all the days of their lives.*
>
> *Yiii-eeee, Nyarlathotep! Lord of Death!*

Still facing the orange rod of the altar, touch the key of Nyarlathotep to your forehead, kiss it reverently, and press it to your heart center beneath your hands.

Close your eyelids and use the power of your will to draw up from the fathomless depths beneath the altar triangle the orange ray of Nyarlathotep, so that its astral light floods the circle and concentrates itself in the air above the altar.

Meditate for a minute or two on the power of Nyarlathotep to torment and destroy the souls of those who displease him or oppose the will of the Old Ones, and on his quick intelligence, which is able to understand any puzzle or mechanism.

Open your eyes and walk around the circle widdershins to stand before the orange stone of Nyarlathotep. Tap it with the key and speak the words:

The circle is broken!

As you do so, visualize the orange rays that link the stones into a heptagon break apart on either side of the orange stone and vanish. Circumambulate widdershins to stand facing the blue rod at the base of the altar. Place the key of Nyarlathotep into the altar. Stand in silent meditation for a minute or so to clear your thoughts. Extinguish the altar lights to end the ritual, put away your sash and lamen of Nyar-lathotep, along with the wrapped Elder Seal, and carefully discard any prayers or offerings to the lord that occupied the triangle during the ritual.

Rite of Yog-Sothoth
(Thursday)

The wrapped Elder Seal is placed in the altar triangle, along with the circular key of Yog-Sothoth and any prayers or offerings to the god. Yog-Sothoth is lord of the heights and of gates, and is associated with the sphere of Jupiter, so appropriate offerings would include such things as mirrors that are a kind of doorway, wine that opens the mind, strong incense that is not too sweet, eagle or hawk feathers, turquoise, blue crystals and gems, pennants, flags, streamers, pinwheels, balloons, and old door keys.

Wearing the lamen of Yog-Sothoth around your neck and the blue sash of the lord around your waist, light the flames at the points of the altar and stand facing the blue rod at the base of the triangle. Speak the words that open the ritual:

On this day of Yog-Sothoth, I invoke the Lord of Gates.

Pick up the circular key of Yog-Sothoth from the altar in your right hand and walk widdershins around the circle to the blue stone. Strike the stone gently with the key and make a complete circumambulation around the circle, moving against the course of the sun, and touching the stones of the circle as you pass them, so that you return to the stone of Yog-Sothoth. Strike the blue stone a second time to complete and seal the circle. Speak these words:

The circle is joined!

On the astral level, visualize blue rays of light linking the seven stones of the circle to form a heptagon with the stones at its points.

Walk widdershins around the circle until you reach the blue rod at the base of the altar triangle. This rod is the threshold of the Gate of the Heights, which belongs especially to Yog-Sothoth. All gates are gates of Yog-Sothoth, but through the Gate of the Heights is the presence of the sky god himself invoked.

Extend the key of Yog-Sothoth in your right hand across the blue threshold rod on the altar, and angle it sharply upward so that it points high above the center of the altar. Recite the litany of Yog-Sothoth:

Lofty Yog-Sothoth, ruler of all portals, opener of the way, keeper of the threshold, lord of coming and going, god of transitions between worlds, you who are both the gate and the key, who were called Janus by the Romans, who guards the ways to the black throne of chaos, approach this stone circle through the Gate of the Heights.

Receive this offering as a tribute of respect and fidelity. Confer good fortune on all who stand within this circle, and all who observe this rite. Heed the prayers of those who have placed offerings upon the altar. Bless the works of the Order of the Old Ones that are done in your name, and in the names of the seven lords. Send your agents to watch over and protect all who serve you this day, and all the days of their lives.

Yiii-eeee, Yog-Sothoth! Lord of Gates!

As you continue to stand facing the blue threshold rod at the base of the altar, touch the key of Yog-Sothoth to your forehead, kiss the key and press it to your heart center beneath both your hands. Close your eyes, and with the force of your will draw down from the heights above the altar the blue ray of Yog-Sothoth, so that it fills the stone circle with astral radiance, and concentrates itself above the altar triangle.

For a minute or so, meditate upon the power of Yog-Sothoth to both open and seal the gateways between dimensions of reality, and between distant worlds. All gates belong to Yog-Sothoth, from the most humble to the most exotic, and those he chooses to close cannot be passed through.

Open your eyelids and walk widdershins around the circle until you stand before the blue stone of Yog-Sothoth. Strike it gently with the key and speak the words:

The circle is broken!

In your imagination, see the blue rays on either side of the stone wink out of existence on the astral level, causing the heptagon of blue light that joins all the stones to vanish from the circle. Walk around the circle widdershins and stand before the blue rod at the base of the altar. Return the key to the altar. Pause a minute or two in silent meditation to empty your mind and still your emotions.

Put out the altar flames, remove your lamen and sash, and carefully discard any prayers or offerings that were within the triangle, bearing in mind that they have been devoted wholly to Yog-Sothoth and must have no other use.

Rite of Shub-Niggurath
(Friday)

Written prayers and material offerings to Shub-Niggurath should be placed in the triangle of the altar before beginning the ritual. Appropriate offerings include such things as pleasant incense, perfumes, sweets, red wine, body oils, fine soaps, rich fabrics, and in general things that indulge the senses and cause pleasure, particularly pleasures of a sensual or sexual kind. Also on the altar should be put the covered Elder Seal and the key of Shub-Niggurath, which is in the shape of a triangle. When you hold the triangle during rituals devoted to this goddess, you should usually hold it with one point downward, to represent the female vulva. The exception to this rule is in rituals to Shub-Niggurath that invoke her masculine sexual energies, but these masculine energies are not invoked during her day rite.

Wearing the lamen of Shub-Niggurath around your neck and her green sash tied at your waist, light the three flames at the points of the altar. Stand at the base of the triangle facing the blue rod and speak the opening words:

On this day of Shub-Niggurath, I invoke the Lady of Desire.

Take up the triangular key of Shub-Niggurath from the altar and proceed widdershins around the circle to stand beside the green stone of the goddess. Gently strike the stone with the key so that it rings, and make a complete circumambulation around the altar, touching each stone in turn with the key as you pass, and touching the green stone a second time to complete and close the circle. Speak the words:

The circle is joined!

Visualize green rays of light extending between the stones to form a heptagon with the stones at its points. This should be created on the astral level in your imagination, where, if you wish, you may visualize the stones as larger than they are in the physical world, and the rays of green light at the level of your heart center.

Walk around the circle widdershins to stand in the east, facing outward. Extend the key of Shub-Niggurath in your right hand through the stone circle, with its point turned downward, so that the key is directed at the Gate of the East, which is visualized as a translucent rectangle that rises above the green threshold rod beyond the circle in the east. The key is extended at heart level. Recite the litany of Shub-Niggurath:

> *Wanton Shub-Niggurath, whose womb is ever-fruitful, goddess of wild desires and unchecked generation, who brings forth abundantly from the loins of beasts and the furrows of the field, great lady of desires, mistress of glamours, mother of monsters, who is called the Goat With A Thousand Young and the Black Goat of the Wood by witches, who is known as Lilith among the wise, approach this stone circle through the Gate of the East.*
>
> *Receive this offering as a tribute of respect and fidelity. Confer good fortune on all who stand within this circle, and all who observe this rite. Heed the prayers of those who have placed offerings upon the altar. Bless the works of the Order of the Old Ones that are done in your name, and in the names of the seven lords. Send your agents to watch over and protect all who serve you this day, and all the days of their lives.*
>
> *Yiii-eeee, Shub-Niggurath! Lady of Lust!*

Touch the key of Shub-Niggurath to your forehead between your brows, kiss it with reverence, and hold it pressed to your heart center beneath your hands. Close your eyes and visualize a ray of green light pouring through the opened Gate of the East to pass through your body and fill the stone circle with green radiance. The light from the green ray concentrates itself in the air above the altar.

Meditate silently for a minute or two on the power of Shub-Niggurath to excite desire and to give sexual pleasure, and on her endless fertility that can bring forth wholesome fruits of the womb or monsters, depending on how it is channeled and directed.

Open your eyes and proceed widdershins around the circle to stand in front of the green stone of the goddess. Any companions who share the rite with you must walk in the same direction as you walk, taking care to keep the same spacing around the circle. Strike the green stone gently with the key and speak the words:

The circle is broken!

Visualize on the astral level the green rays on either side of the stone wink out, along with the rest of the rays forming the heptagon of light. Walk widdershins around the circle to stand in the south, facing the blue rod at the base of the altar triangle, which is the starting point and ending point of the rite. Put the key back onto the altar. Stand silently for a minute with your back straight and your arms at your sides, until your mind is clear and your emotions calm. This is the time to release any energies aroused by the ritual.

Put out the altar flames, remove your lamen and sash, and discard with reverence and care the prayers and offerings that were dedicated to Shub-Niggurath. She has drawn from them their occult essences, so you must discard the husks.

Rite of Yig
(Saturday)

Any prayers and offerings to Yig should be placed in the triangle shortly before his day rite is conducted. Yig is lord of serpents, and is associated with long life, resistance to disease, wisdom, old age, silence, ancient things, renewal, physical health, and the keeping of oaths. Saturnine things are in general appropriate as offerings, such as black stones, bits of lead, bones, antique objects, bitter roots, strong and harsh incense, and watches or other things associated with time. Beside the offerings is put the Elder Seal, carefully wrapped and bound up in its white cover, and the key of Yig, which has the shape of a lemniscate.

Place the lamen of Yig around your neck and tie his black sash at your waist. If you wear the black robe of the Order for the daily rites, these things are worn on the outside of the robe. Otherwise they are worn over your black ritual clothing. Light the three flames at the points of the altar. Stand in the starting position to the south of the altar, facing the blue rod at its base, and speak the opening words:

On this day of Yig, I invoke the Lord of Ages.

Remove the key of Yig from the altar and walk around the circle widdershins to stand before the black stone of Yig with the altar behind you. Bend and strike the stone of Yig with the key in your right hand, then complete a circumambulation around the altar, touching each stone as you pass with the key so that its metal rings faintly. Touch the black stone a second time to complete and close the circle. As you do so, speak the words:

The circle is joined!

As you stand before the black stone of Yig, visualize on the astral level rays of black light extending between the stones of the circle to form a heptagon with the stones at its points. Black rays are best visualized as flickering with violet light along their edges, which define their shape against a dark background. The black heptagon may be imagined to float upon the air at heart level between the larger stones of the astral circle.

There is no need to walk around the circle to reach the gate associated with Yig. It is the only gate that is directly opposite the stone of its lord. Hold the key of Yig by one of its loops in your right hand and extend it straight out toward the north on the level of your heart, so that it projects through the circle and points at the translucent Gate of the North that rises as a rectangle above the black threshold rod in the north. Recite the following litany of Yig:

> *Ancient Yig, Father of Serpents, oldest of the Old Ones who reside in this lower sphere, who was present at the beginning of things and shall witness the end of days, who was called the Old Serpent by the Hebrews and Apep by the Egyptians, whom some name Damballah, whose sinuous body wraps around the world, who never speaks but only hisses, approach this stone circle through the Gate of the North.*
>
> *Receive this offering as a tribute of respect and fidelity. Confer good fortune on all who stand within this circle, and all who observe this rite. Heed the prayers of those who have placed offerings upon the altar. Bless the works of the Order of the Old Ones that are done in your name, and in the names of the seven lords. Send your agents to watch over and protect all who serve you this day, and all the days of their lives.*
>
> *Yiii-eeee, Yig! Lord of Ages!*

Touch the key of Yig to your forehead, kiss it with reverence, and press it beneath your folded hands to the center of your chest. Close your eyes and will the black ray of Yig to shine outward from the opened Gate of the North and pass through your body to fill the stone circle, concentrating its darkness like a dark mist above the triangle of the altar.

For a minute or two, continue to stand in that pose and meditate silently on the greatness and wisdom of Yig, who safeguards his children from harm, and who keeps his wisdom to himself, never revealing the secrets entrusted to his care. Of all the Old Ones, Yig is best to invoke for protection, but only by those who remain faithful to him.

Open your eyes and strike the key gently against the black stone of Yig at your feet. There is no need to move around the circle to reach the stone, which is directly in front of the Gate of the North. Speak the words:

The circle is broken!

Visualize on the astral level the black rays on either side of the black stone of Yig wink out of existence, as the heptagon of black light vanishes from the circle.

Walk widdershins around the altar to stand in the south facing north, with the blue rod at the base of the altar triangle in front of you. Replace the key of Yig on the triangle. Bow your head for a minute to clear your thoughts and still your emotions. Then extinguish the altar lights and remove the lamen and sash of Yig. Discard with care any prayers or offerings to Yig that may be on the altar.

Rite of Azathoth
(Sunday)

Azathoth is associated with the sphere of the sun, although in an occluded manner, as when the sun is in eclipse behind the moon, as well as with all vortices, spirals, and whirlwinds. Offerings that may be placed on the altar as gifts to this lord include objects of gold or yellow brass, yellow stones and gems, spiral things such as metal springs and spiral flowers, pendulums, spinning tops, wheels, honey, beeswax, and things connected with music and the making of music, such as guitar strings or guitar picks, whistles, or bells. Beside any offerings and written prayers to Azathoth, put his key and the Elder Seal wrapped and tied in its protective covering.

Hang the lamen of Azathoth around your neck on its chain or cord, and tie his yellow sash to your waist so that its ends dangle down on the left side. Light the three flames of the altar to empower it. Stand at the south of the altar, facing the blue rod that forms its base, and utter the words of opening:

On this day of Azathoth, I invoke the Lord of Creation.

Remove the spiral key of Azathoth from the altar and go a short distance around the circle widdershins to stand before the yellow stone with the altar at your back. Strike the stone of Azathoth with the key and complete a full circumambulation against the course of the sun, touching the key to each stone in the circle as you pass so that the key gives forth ringing tones. Strike it gently against the yellow stone a second time in order to complete and seal the circle. Speak the words:

The circle is joined!

Visualize yellow rays linking all seven stones, so that they form the points of a heptagon of yellow light. On the astral plane, see the stones standing higher, with the rays from their tips at the level of your heart.

Walk around the circle widdershins to stand facing the yellow rod on the right side of the triangular altar. Hold the spiral key out in your right hand so that it extends across the yellow threshold rod and is centered above the altar. The gate of Azathoth is the Gate of the Center, so be sure that your arm is not angled noticeably upward or downward. Recite the following litany of Azathoth:

Blind Azathoth, center of chaos, called the idiot god by fools but lord of creation and destruction by the wise, who occupies the central seat of the black throne, who pipes the music of making and unmaking, about whom the twelve elder gods forever dance, whose true name cannot be spoken but who is the Alpha and Omega of the Greeks, approach this stone circle through the Gate of the Center.

Receive this offering as a tribute of respect and fidelity. Confer good fortune on all who stand within this circle, and all who observe this rite. Heed the prayers of those who have placed offerings upon the altar. Bless the works of the Order of the Old Ones that are done in your name, and in the names of the seven lords. Send your agents to watch over and protect all who serve you this day, and all the days of their lives.

Yiii-eeee, Azathoth! Lord of Existence!

Touch the key to your forehead, kiss it, and press it to the center of your chest. Close your eyes and, with the power of your will, draw forth from the air above the center of the altar the expanding golden ray of Azathoth so that it fills the stone circle with its radiance. This yellow light is most concentrated above the altar itself. It does not emanate in the form of a ray, but as an expanding sphere.

Meditate for a minute or two on the sorrow of Azathoth, who is the ever-turning wheel of both creation and destruction, the revolving vortex at the heart of chaos, which became darkened by the fall from grace of the goddess Barbelzoa.

Open your eyes and go around the circle widdershins to stand before the yellow stone. Strike it gently with the key. Speak the words:

The circle is broken!

Visualize the yellow rays of light that extend on either side of the yellow stone wink out of existence. All the stones of the circle are disconnected as the yellow heptagon vanishes on the astral level.

Walk around the altar counterclockwise so that you stand in the south of the circle, facing the blue rod that forms the base of the altar triangle. Replace the key of Azathoth on the altar, and take a minute to empty your mind and release your emotions. Put out the three altar flames. Take off the lamen and yellow sash of Azathoth. Discard with care the prayers and offerings to Azathoth that may reside on the altar.

Book of the West Gate:
Attainment

Way of Yig

The discipline of Yig is one of physical control and self-denial. Yig is the Old Serpent, ancient and wise. All serpents slide along the ground on their bellies, so their awareness is always focused on material matters. For this reason they were linked to the health and life cycles of the body. Through his sphere of Saturn, Yig presides especially over the health of the body in its densest form, the bones. He rules the foundations of physical well-being, and is concerned with the material essentials of life, such as drink, food, and exercise.

The serpent is a symbol of the Greek god of medicine, Asclepius, because the serpent was believed in ancient times to be able to cyclically renew itself, and in this way to defy death forever. Each time a snake shed its skin, the ancients believed that it was renewing its youth, banishing all disease and infirmity in the process. The way of Yig is a way of perpetual renewal.

Masters who walk the path of Yig to the base of the chaos mount must concern themselves with physical exercise, diet, and the health of the body. It is a path that demands discipline and self-control. Physical indulgence or excess cannot be tolerated. It is a path of balance. The awareness remains keenly focused on the condition of the body at all times, to a degree that would be considered obsessive by the uninitiated.

Regular daily exercise is used to strengthen the body and increase physical endurance. This should include both light weight training and aerobic training. Excess of any kind should be shunned, including excess in any particular area of training. If the body complains through pain, it should be heeded, and the exercise routine changed to give time for the injured part of the body to heal itself. However, if possible the training should never be stopped once it is begun. Even during periods of sickness such as colds or the flu, light physical training should be continued, if it is possible to do so without serious health risks.

At the same time this exercise regime is being carried forward, attention must be given to what is taken into the body to nourish it. Wherever possible, drugs, alcohol, and highly spiced foods should be eliminated, or at least reduced. The intake of meat should generally be reduced—this does not apply to those who are already on a meat-free or meat-reduced diet. In place of red meat, fish or poultry should be frequently substituted, to lighten the stress on the digestive system. The aim is to purify the body, while providing ample calories and nutrients to sustain regular physical exercise. Foods that sit heavily in the stomach, such as meat-filled pastries or sausage, should be avoided.

It is not necessary to give up particular foods, but those that demand more involvement of the body should be reduced. Foods that are craved should be reduced, since the body often craves what is unhealthy for it. Sugar, salt, grease, and caffeine should all be drastically cut down or eliminated from the average diet.

A little chilled but unsweetened lime or lemon juice should be taken immediately after rising in the morning on an empty stomach. This encourages perspiration. It is useful to do a simple exercise routine immediately after drinking this juice that consists of sitting postures or stretching exercises. Physical yoga is one of vehicles on the way of Yig. Of all creatures, the serpent is the most flexible, and the flexibility that is the goal of yoga is in keeping with the philosophy of Yig. It is not absolutely necessary for those who follow the path of Yig to learn yoga postures, but those who turn their backs on yoga will have a much more difficult time in attaining the black throne.

Expertise in yoga is not required. It is enough that a set of postures be performed daily without fail, and that they be done with serious concentration of both mind and body. The morning yoga practice should be done without distractions such as music or conversation. It is best to work in solitude and in silence. Silence is the way of Yig. The serpent is voiceless. Listen to your body.

After the morning yoga or stretching routine, it is good to sit and meditate on the greatness and wisdom of Yig in the form of the great serpent that encircles the world. It is this great serpent that defines the boundaries of the known from the unknown, of cosmos from chaos. To cross the path of this serpent is to progress to the black throne.

Those who walk the path of Yig adore this lord as their benevolent and loving father, knowing that Yig is a generous god who showers good fortune on his children. He is also mighty in their defense. Woe to those who injure the children of Yig, who are his disciples on the path of attainment. He strikes with poison those who defy him, and crushes his foes to death in his myriad and bewildering coils, which never cease to weave and flow and slide over each other. Meditate upon the endless movement in the sinuous coiled body of Yig.

The exercises to strengthen the muscles and increase endurance are done later in the day, at a convenient hour. They should be done at the same time each day, and the exercise session should not be omitted. When an initiate begins to walk the path of Yig, numerous petty distractions will arise to beguile the mind and interrupt the training, but these should be strenuously denied and resisted. Those who choose this way of attainment must commit themselves completely to its working, in the realization that the austerities of Yig are the most important matters in their lives. Only through this dedication to the way will they attain the ninety-three steps of the black throne mount.

The way of Yig requires scrupulous physical cleanliness and attention to grooming. Hair should be cut short or worn in such a way that it does not fall loosely. Jewelry should not be worn to excess, but if adopted at all must be in harmony with Yig. Serpentine patterns and chains in silver and jet are appropriate. Black semi-precious stones such as obsidian or jet, and black pearls, are generally appropriate. Black clothing is in keeping with the occult correspondences of Yig, but need not be worn exclusively. All these outward details of appearance are reminders of Yig, and of the importance of following his path with fidelity.

Masters who have committed themselves to the way of Yig may wish to get the seal of this lord of the Old Ones tattooed in black ink on their skin, as a token of their dedication to this path. It also serves to indicate to other initiates of the Order the path that is being followed. A tattoo of the seal of Yig should only be adopted where there is total commitment to the way of that lord, for to wear his seal but to defy and show contempt for his path will unfailingly arouse the anger of the lord, and bring misfortune upon the head of the fool who has wandered from the way. The tattoo, if adopted, should be modest in size and in its placement on the body. In place of a tattoo, the emblem of Yig, which is a knotted cord or noose, may be worn on the clothing.

Once on each cycle of the moon, a Master who seeks to walk the way of Yig may conduct the ritual of opening, in which the North Gate of Yig is unsealed by the agency of Yog-Sothoth, and Nyarlathotep is invoked to act as a guide along the path to the black throne. Prior to conducting this ritual of opening the gate, the disciple of Yig should fast for a full cycle of the day and night, taking only modest amounts of water, tea, or fruit juices. In this way the body is lightened and purified. A prolonged period of meditation on Yig and his path should be done prior to attempting the ritual of opening, which is conducted commencing at midnight on the night of the waxing half-moon, when the lunar orb is bright on the right side and dark on the left side.

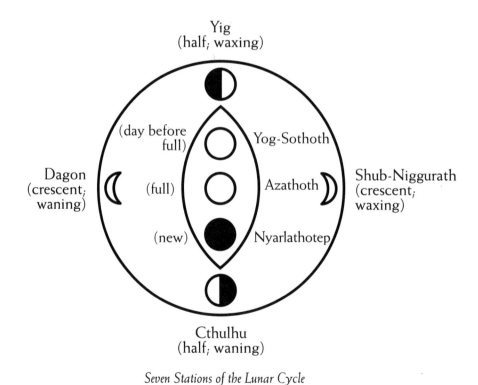

Seven Stations of the Lunar Cycle

If the ritual of opening succeeds, Nyarlathotep will lead the disciple along the way of Yig on the astral level, while the disciple sits passively in his physical body within the stone circle. The disciple will sign his name in the *Necronomicon* while in his astral shell and will swear allegiance either to Azathoth or to his messenger Nyarlathotep, as he chooses. If the ritual fails to achieve consummation, it may be conducted again on the following waxing half-moon, and so on as often as is required to achieve a successful completion of the path.

The newly ascended Lord of the Order who has successfully walked the way of Yig remains bound to Yig, and should continue to observe the discipline of Yig, although its rigors may be reduced. Those who are true disciples of Yig will not wish to give up his practices, for these will seem the fittest way of life. Just as the seal of Yig, once tattooed on the skin, cannot be casually removed, so the way of Yig cannot be casually discontinued.

The emblem carried by those who walk the way of Yig is the corded noose, which represents the suppleness of the serpent. It may be worn about the neck as a fine cord so that the tail of the noose hangs down the chest, or may be worn on the wrist or ankle. The cord should be black in color, its knots elaborate in design to indicate the subtlety of Yig. Alternatively, a piece of jewelry such as a brooch or pendant that is in the form of an elaborate knot may be worn.

Way of Shub-Niggurath

The way of Shub-Niggurath is the way of sensual experience and sexual arousal, sustained and heightened to such a degree that it alters consciousness. It is best followed with the aid of a partner, since most sexuality is shared with other human beings. Sexual experience alone is not enough, however. To walk this path is to create an environment of sensual pleasure that functions through all five senses, and spans the spectrum of sensation from the most grossly physical acts of sexual release to the most sublime heights of artistic enjoyment.

A living environment must be created that excludes anything unpleasant or discordant. The seeker must submerge himself in sights, sounds, smells, tastes, and tactile sensations that give various levels of pleasure. This should be sustained as far as is possible throughout the day and night. Harsh or violent sense impressions should be avoided. The seeker on this path must strive to steep the soul in beauty of all kinds, particularly beauty of a sensual kind that provokes arousal. An attempt should be made to refine and render increasingly sensitive the aesthetic judgment by an appreciation of art and music. Care should be taken to choose only elegant and attractive clothing, to speak in a gentle yet witty manner, to excite the palate with unusual but pleasant foods and drinks.

The mind must be turned to the fertile goddess. Her image should be before the inner sight of the aspirant, who must carry on an interior communication with Shub-Niggurath as one lover would speak in a familiar way to another. Prayers and blessings should be offered to Shub-Niggurath. Thanks should be given to the goddess when a beautiful image or sensual pleasure is experienced.

On the day prior to the attempt to open the Gate of the East upon the path to the black throne, the follower of this way should rely on the aid of a partner to sustain his arousal without interruption continuously. This can be done with the aid of caresses, embraces, erotic art, sensual music, incense, sensual baths, and oils for the skin. If necessary, the aspirant may sustain his own arousal, but this is more difficult as it divides concentration. Always the image of Shub-Niggurath should be held in the imagination, but in a form of the goddess that is attractive and seductive to the aspirant for her favor. Female disciples will choose to conceive her in her masculine aspect, unless they favor the love of women.

While this sustained arousal is being maintained on the day prior to the ritual of opening the gate, the follower of this path must not sleep. Fatigue of the senses is necessary to open the Gate of the East. Arousal should be maintained to a condition of discomfort that is almost painful. If Shub-Niggurath has heard and heeded the prayers of the aspirant, the goddess will help to sustain arousal, sometimes to a degree that seems almost superhuman. To the follower of her path, she is a lover—not an equal lover, but a superior lover who condescends to share her blessing with those who worship her.

It may seem that the way of Shub-Niggurath is easier and more agreeable than the ways of the other lords of the Old Ones. This is an illusion. It is true that the discipline of her path is milder and more pleasant than that of other paths, but by its very nature it distracts the mind away from the higher purpose of the attainment of the black throne. It is easy to become lost in sensation and the enjoyment of sexual play. To allow the methods of this path to become the goal is fatal to success. All too easily the discipline of sensual arousal may devolve into mere satisfaction.

Because the path is so difficult, consummation of arousal must be avoided. The purpose is altered consciousness through arousal, not through orgasm. To achieve orgasm is to fail on this path. Instead, the desire is heightened in every possible way, the sexual arousal is made as intense and as sustained as the human body can withstand, and is held at this level, but orgasm, which ends arousal, is shunned. Orgasm is a sly deceiver on this path, who steals away purpose and leads the follower of the way of Shub-Niggurath into snares and pitfalls.

The goddess will have a secret image and form that she will use to those who worship her and follower her way. It is unique to each worshipper. In this form she comes as a lover and plays with her disciples. These visits, which occur most often in dreams, but may also happen during states of sustained arousal, are to be welcomed, for during her visits the goddess reveals secrets to those who love her. The followers of her path are often prophets who receive revelations during sleep.

Shub-Niggurath is the same as the Hebrew goddess Lilith, who has many forms both lovely and terrible. She is the goddess Shakti of the Hindus, the source of all manifest power in the universe, as expressed by her ever-fertile womb that never ceases to bring forth new creations. Those who follow her way will have good success if they use some of the same techniques of the worshippers of Shakti on the left-hand path of sensual indulgence. They may also employ techniques of Lilith worship with fruitful results.

The night of the lunar cycle of the moon devoted to the opening of the Gate of the East is the third night following the night of the new moon, when the moon appears in the heavens shortly after sunset as a slender waxing crescent. The ritual is conducted at midnight so that the sun is on the far side of the world, and its influence is reduced to its lowest ebb. Since the hours of the day begin at midnight, the ritual must be commenced at the beginning of the first hour of the third day of the lunar cycle after the new moon. If the mind and body of the disciple of Shub-Niggurath have been perfected, his heightened consciousness will induce Yog-Sothoth to open the Gate of the East, and Nyarlathotep will come to lead the way to the black throne.

If the attempt to open the gate on the path fails, as is often the case on the first attempt, and even on the eleventh attempt for those unfortunates who do not adhere with serious mind and steadfast heart to the regime of the goddess, another attempt may be made on the following lunar cycle.

Those who walk the path of Shub-Niggurath are her lovers. They may wish to have her seal tattooed on their skin as a sign of fidelity to her sensual and artistic way of attainment. Even after they reach the black throne and inscribe their name in the *Necronomicon*, they remain devoted to her more so than to any of the other lords. To walk the path of a lord of the Old Ones is to become the disciple of that lord, which is why the choice of a path is so important and should never be rashly made.

The physical emblem of this path is the rose, a flower of intimacy and sensuality. It should be worn by the followers of the discipline of Shub-Niggurath somewhere on their body or on their clothing, if they do not adopt the tattoo of her seal. Either the flower itself may be carried, or a piece of jewelry worked into the form of a rose may be worn. The emblem is a kind of badge of service that alerts other members of the Order to the way chosen by the Master, and should be worn in a place that is visible for this reason.

Way of Cthulhu

Of all the lords of the Old Ones, mighty Cthulhu is the greatest warrior. His innumerable spawn, who are smaller off-buddings of himself, are his army, and have the same capacity to reform their gelatinous bodies after injuries, so that they are virtually deathless and in the common course of events eternal. Only when utterly annihilated, as may occur in confrontation with a shoggoth when they are wholly engulfed and consumed, do they cease to exist. Those who follow the way of this lord imitate his spawn and study the art of war and the techniques of battle. They are obedient to his will as are soldiers to the will of their general.

The discipline of Cthulhu requires strengthening the will and hardening the body for combat. Martial arts and methods of fighting must be studied. The particular fighting style that is adopted is unimportant. It is only required that the disciple on the way of this lord steep himself in the ways of battle. In addition to daily training in unarmed fighting techniques, the disciple should study the use of personal weapons such as the knife and the gun, and should become familiar both with their workings and their use.

No Master should attempt to walk this path who does not possess an innate fascination for fighting and for warfare. This is the way of the warrior. Cthulhu favors the brave and the devoted. He looks with scorn upon those who are timid and have not the heart to endure the rigors of his discipline. To the victorious in battle he sends good fortune, but to those who strive and fail he is less generous, and those who flee from combat earn only his disfavor and should avoid all attempts to invoke him as his disciples.

Training for this way involves physical exercise to strengthen and harden the body, mock combat to hone the skills of the warrior, and the study of fighting techniques and the use of weapons. Boxing is a useful method of training. Actual full-contact sparring against opponents that tests the proficiency of the disciple is essential. Success in training cannot be assumed without trial by combat. Eastern fighting arts are also useful for their rigorous exercises and the hardships they impose on the body. Military training of the kind that is given to new recruits is suitable for this path.

The physical training on the way of Yig is intended to make the body healthy, flexible, and perfect in its balance and beauty. The disciple of Yig seeks the sinuous body of a dancer. By contrast, the physical training of Cthulhu must achieve a hardening of the flesh, so that it can endure blows and abuse with indifference. The disciple of Cthulhu seeks the body of a champion.

In addition to physical conditioning, the will must be hardened and honed to a sharp edge, so that it is equal to all challenges and can pierce through doubts and confusion. It is useful to pray to Cthulhu for courage and strength both of the body and of the mind while walking this martial path. Cthulhu will not turn away from those who invoke him with a sincere and steadfast heart. Although he lies sleeping beneath the waves, and cannot send his thoughts outward unaided, those who seek him through prayers and invocations are able to reach his dreaming mind, which extends to meet them. In this way the lord of war can find his disciples in their dreams, where he teaches them courage and fortitude.

An image of Cthulhu should be maintained persistently before the inner sight of those who walk his path. When it becomes vague, it must be renewed in the imagination. Frequent prayers of praise and thanksgiving should be spoken in the name of this lord, and when difficulties arise, his disciples should call upon him for courage and strength. He will stand with those who are bold of heart.

At some point in the training for this path, the disciple of Cthulhu will be tested and will either emerge from the test victorious, or will fail. Failure is not fatal in itself, but may merely be a way for the lord of battle to harden the will of his true followers by showing them the bitterness of defeat. Those who fail are tested more rigorously than those who achieve victory. If their will is not broken, they emerge the stronger for it. The discipline of Cthulhu is not for the weak, nor for the faint of heart.

The night of the lunar cycle on which the ritual to open the Gate of the South on the path to the black throne may be conducted is the third quarter, when the waning face of the moon is half illuminated, bright on the left side and dark on the right. The ritual is begun at midnight, as the day of the third quarter commences. If the first attempt does not succeed in opening the gate, the true warrior of Cthulhu will persevere until all obstacles are overcome and the gate yields. Without fear the disciple will pass through in the astral body and confront waiting Nyarlathotep, who will lead the way to the steps of the chaos mount.

Masters who choose to walk this path remain soldiers of Cthulhu, and may wish to have his seal tattooed somewhere upon their skin as a mark of their dedication to the way of the warrior. The seal tattoo is a choice, not a requirement, and is left to the judgment of those who walk the paths of the seven lords. The disciples of Cthulhu serve the Order as guards and when necessary, as enforcers of discipline, or to defend the temples against foes. The other members of the Order, regardless of their rank, should look to the disciples of Cthulhu for aid and protection. To walk this difficult path is a noble attainment.

The emblem of this path is a dagger or other edged weapon. It may be either practical or symbolic. For example, a folding knife may be worn exposed at the belt, or a pin or pendant in the shape of a dagger or sword may be worn as jewelry. The emblem indicates to other members of the Order those who are the disciples of Cthulhu. For this reason it should always be visible to others.

Way of Dagon

The Gate of the West is opened on the path to the black throne by following the way of Dagon, which is a discipline of study and scholarship, particularly involving the arcane arts or ceremonial or high magic of past ages. All serious scholars of religion and magic walk the path of Dagon, whether they know it or not. Through the acquisition and analysis of abstruse knowledge, the mind is transformed and rendered fit to open the West Gate.

Through the acquisition of knowledge and the exercise of reasoning, the perception of reality is altered. A deeper and more meaningful awareness of the universe and the human place in it is attained. Reality as we know it arises in the mind. By transforming the mind, reality is transformed. By controlling the mind, reality is controlled. By commanding the mind, reality is commanded.

Among the lords of the Old Ones, Dagon is the greatest scholar. Although Yig keeps more ancient secrets, and Nyarlathotep is more crafty, the learning of Dagon is as vast as the oceans in which he dwells. His children, the Deep Ones, excel in metallurgy and the crafting of fine cloths and jewelry. They are artisans and architects beyond compare. Their statuary is as fine as any carved by the ancient Greeks. Their stone monuments defy time. It was their gift of energy rays to the aristocratic rulers of Atlantis that led to the destruction of that island empire, when the rays were misused in civil war.

The studies of those who walk this path will vary from disciple to disciple according to natural inclination, but they must seek to be proficient in astrology and in the mythologies of Persia, Egypt, and Greece, in the Kabbalah of the Hebrews and the teachings of the Gnostics, in spiritual alchemy and in the understanding of occult symbols, in the teachings of the Platonists and the Pythagoreans, in the books of Hermes Trismegistus, and in the tarot. The way of Dagon is the way of the wizard, a word derived from the word "wise." His disciples must know the angels of Enoch and their calls, and the hierarchies of heaven.

Not all of this knowledge is necessary to open the West Gate, but all of it is desirable in a true child of Dagon. It is the process of study, of stretching and opening the mind, that allows the alteration of consciousness that will open the gate. No one may predict which area of study will provide the key to the gate. The seeker should study those subjects that most strongly engage the interest. The mind knows what it needs, and will acquire the necessary skills if given the opportunity. Be guided in your studies by the inner voice of Dagon, who will speak to you in your dreams.

The danger on this path is to become so obsessed with the acquisition of facts that the capacity for learning is stunted. Only when the mind remains uncertain of what it knows can new knowledge be acquired. An arrogant mind is a closed mind, and a mind closed can never open the gate. The seeker should embrace uncertainty, and run after any teaching that throws his thoughts into chaos. When he feels his reason slipping away, and the very ground of reality turn to sand and begin to shift under his feet, he is approaching the necessary condition of mind to open the West Gate.

Challenge everything! Never assume a thing is so, but turn it on its head and see the truth that is inherent in its opposite. A mental condition must be cultivated in which no matter is perceived as either true, or not true, but is seen to be both true and untrue simultaneously. This is the practice of Zen, where the certain is cut away bit by bit until only uncertainty remains—but before it can be cut away, it must be acquired. There is value in the ancient learning. The disciple of the West Gate must see its truth, see its falsity, and yet see both at the same time without conflict.

In this way the perspective of the mind is elevated above the mundane to the sublime, and Dagon begins to interest himself in the progress of his disciple. Dagon cares nothing for those who are sure of their wisdom. He embraces in his finny grasp only those who are sure that they know nothing. In loss there is gain. In uncertainty comes truth. When the mind is filled, and then emptied, the gate is opened. Unless the disciple of Dagon is looked upon by other members of the Order as more than half-mad, he has made no progress on his chosen path.

The night of the lunar cycle given to the ritual of opening the Gate of the West is the third night before the night of the new moon, when the waning lunar crescent is as thin as a bow, and rises late in the east. The ritual should be begun at the midnight hour that commences that third night before the darkness of the moon. If the mind of the disciple is ready, Yog-Sothoth will open the gate and Nyarlathotep will stand waiting to escort the scholar of Dagon safely through the dangers along the path to the foot of the chaos mount.

Thos who follow the path of Dagon may wish to wear his seal tattooed in black ink upon their skin, as a token of their respect and loyalty. If they prefer, they should carry the emblem of this lord on their persons at all times when they are in the presence of strangers, for it is a proclamation of their chosen path of attainment. The emblem of Dagon is the book or scroll, which may be an actual book, or the symbolic representation of a book. The ancient practice of wearing a written prayer rolled up inside a small ornate cylinder of silver, which is then hung on a chain around the neck and serves as a pendant, is admirably fit for the emblem of Dagon.

Way of Yog-Sothoth

The ways of the three inner gates differ from the ways of the four outer gates in forcing the seeker to turn inward. The outer gates are approached through the manipulation of physical externals: body training and posture for the North Gate, sensuality and sexual excess for the East Gate, dominance and martial discipline for the South Gate, and the acquisition of knowledge for the West Gate. The first of the inner gates is the Upper Gate of Yog-Sothoth, which is associated with the direction of the heights. Yog-Sothoth is the great gatekeeper of the cosmos. Those who walk his path in search of the black throne do so through the perfection of scrying and astral projection.

Astral projection is an inward discipline since the astral planes cannot be found through outward travel, but only when the mind journeys toward the center, as it does during dreams. The disciples of Yog-Sothoth will be those Masters who have shown a natural talent for seeing visions, and for separating the subtle body from its shell of flesh. Both skills involve the opening of gateways, and are related. In scrying, distant scenes of the astral world are viewed as though through a window, whereas in astral projection the subtle shell of the disciple of Yog-Sothoth seems to travel through a door to be present at those scenes.

This difference is merely a matter of perception. The astral planes are inner realities, and no travel through space is needed to reach them. In scrying the astral world is a painting; in projection the astral world is a stage play. It often happens that a vision will transform itself into an astral setting that surrounds the viewer, as the window becomes the doorway.

Those who scry are useful to the Order, since they possess the ability to divine future events and to peer into secrets and mysteries. There are four traditional mediums for scrying, each in harmony with one of the four lower elements. It is best to select one of these elemental mediums and persist in using it, unless it becomes obvious through repeated failure that it is the wrong element for the person using it. Then, another element should be tried. However, the disciple of Yog-Sothoth must avoid jumping from one element to another capriciously. Find the element that resonates with your own inner nature.

Scrying by fire involves gazing at flickering flames, glowing embers, or the flame of a lamp or candle, as a way of abstracting the mind and opening the window on the astral world. Any glowing source of light can be used to focus the attention, but open flame is the traditional source.

Scrying by water in its most ancient form is the use of a silver basin or crystal bowl filled with water as a kind of mirror in which the astral images reveal themselves. Also under this element is scrying by means of mirrors and crystal globes, which are both watery by their natures. Also involved in this elemental class is the sound of voices or other noises heard in running water or in waves.

Scrying by air uses rising smoke and the scent of incense, tobacco, or some other fuming substance to abstract the mind. It produces a kind of daydream in which visions are viewed. Scrying by air may also be done by gazing at clouds. It sometimes involves the perception of sounds or voices heard on the wind.

Scrying by earth is the casting of lots of different kinds for sortilege. In the pattern in which the lots fall can be discerned images. Divination by tarot is of this type, since it relies on the order of cards dealt after they have been shuffled. So, too, is divination by tea leaves, and geomancy, which relies on the random marking of points in the ground to determine the geomantic signs that are interpreted.

Projection of the astral form can be done during dreams, in which awareness is regained and the dreamer takes control of his will and begins to move freely within the dream, and beyond the dream. By those possessed of sufficient natural ability, it can also be done during waking, while lying on the back on a bed or rug, and then it seems that the astral body rises and separates itself from the physical body.

The astral body does not move through the physical world, however. It moves through a world of its own substance, an astral world in which astral scenes are viewed and entered. This may at times appear identical to the physical world, so that the traveler is deceived into the belief that he travels across space on the material plane. This is illusion. All astral travel is on the astral planes. How could it be otherwise? The astral body cannot enter the physical world, nor can the physical body enter the astral world.

Since all transition through the gates is astral, except in the most exalted and potent of circumstances, which are rarely to be encountered during the course of an entire lifetime, it might be assumed that the way of the Upper Gate is the quickest and best approach to the black throne. This is untrue. A disciple of Yog-Sothoth may undertake numerous astral journeys and never meet Nyarlathotep, and without the guidance of Nyarlathotep, it is impossible to find the black throne amid the innumerable astral planes. It is true that the opening of a gate is almost always an astral event—but skill in astral projection alone does not guarantee the black throne. It is but one of seven disciplines, each of which may lead to attainment if diligently pursued.

.When the disciple of Yog-Sothoth feels ready to attempt the opening of the Gate of the Heights, it should be done on the night of the lunar cycle just prior to the night of the full moon. The ritual of opening is begun at midnight, at the start of the day before the day of the full moon. On this day of each lunar cycle, Yog-Sothoth is exalted, and the barriers between realities thin. If the Gate of the Heights fails to open, or Nyarlathotep fails to present himself as guide to the chaos seat, the ritual may be attempted again on the night just prior to the night of the full moon of the next lunar cycle.

Those who follow the way of Yog-Sothoth may wish to adopt his seal as a tattoo, to proclaim their devotion to his teachings and his service. Or, they may prefer to wear the emblem of this lord of the Old Ones, which is a key, or the representation of a key in the form of jewelry. If a true key is worn, the best kind to choose is a door key since it represents the opening of portals. An antique door key makes an attractive pendant.

Way of Nyarlathotep

The discipleship of Nyarlathotep that opens the Gate of the Depths is one of communication with the spirits of the dead and the underworld. Nyarlathotep is god of the dead and of necromancy. It is an inward path that involves the practice of invocation, but concerns those planes of the astral realm that are chthonic, belonging to darkness and decay. It is the way of the grave and of dead things. Spirits of men and women who have died, but not wholly departed, and other spiritual creatures who were never human, are summoned from the underworld for the purpose of acquiring their knowledge or service.

Men dwell in the middle realm. Yog-Sothoth presides over the astral planes of the heights, being a god of the upper air, and Nyarlathotep rules the astral planes of the depths. In truth there is no height or depth in the astral world, which does not occupy space, but it is convenient to distinguish the celestial and chthonic realms in this manner. It is one of Nyarlathotep's functions to escort the dead to their dark caverns, where they restlessly await the final dissolution of their shells, when they will be caught up like leaves in the whirlwind of the chaos vortex that forever circles the black throne. The decay of the flesh is only one kind of decay. After it comes the decay of the subtle body, and with it the human identity. The older a shade of the dead becomes, the less he remembers of his earthly existence, but the greater his power grows over both the dead and the living.

Ghosts of the dead are the army of Nyarlathotep. They go everywhere, see everything, hear everything. They feed on the life-force of the living things, or on the newly dead from whom the heat has not yet departed. They walk our nightmares in tormented guise, filled with pain and despair and anger. Those dead the longest are recognized as demons, for all humanity has departed from them, and they have forgotten their former names. When a shade of the dead forgets its name, it loses all traces of its human identity. Yet it may acquire or be given a new name, a demonic name that has power over it. Necromancy is concerned with the names of the dead, for in their names lies power over these restless spirits.

Dead souls, demons, and other dead things that were never human lack volition to act for their own purposes. The necromancer supplies the purpose and direction for their actions in the middle realm, just as he supplies the heat and blood that animates them. If he is wise, he does not use his own blood, except in dire necessity, for a shade that consumes the blood of the necromancer acquires power over him. If it consumes enough blood, the necromancer may become its thrall. Shades should be fed on animal blood or on milk. Red meat that is raw may be used as an offering in place of blood when summoning the shades up from the depths. When milk is used, it is best if it is first warmed. Whiskey or other strong spirits can also be used, for they contain heat and fire latent within them.

It may be assumed that the best way to induce Nyarlathotep to lead the way to the black throne is by practicing his discipline of necromancy. This is not so. The way of the underworld is fraught with perils. The dead are deceivers, and the older dead who have forgotten their names and become demons are strong in evil. They delight to trick and betray those who think to use them as servants, and they are forever hungry. No sacrifice is large enough to sate the elder dead. The more they feed, the stronger they become, and the brighter the light of their awareness grows. With it grows their hunger, so that they are more dangerous after receiving the sacrifice. Yet the sacrifice is necessary to make them aware and kindle their strength, so that they can be induced to act for the necromancer's own ends.

Nyarlathotep heeds his worshippers no more than he heeds those who follow the other paths to the throne of chaos. He may choose to answer their prayers, or he may choose to disregard them. He is capricious in his moods, and quick to anger. Woe to any man who calls him when he is angered, for that man has not long to live. He comes to Masters of the Order when they succeed in opening their chosen gates, which they can only do when their minds have been prepared and they have attained the transformed state that permits them to approach the black throne. There are no shortcuts from the path, only precipices and barren wastes.

Those who summon the shades of the dead to visible appearance do so within the altar triangle at the center of the stone circle. Offerings pleasing to the dead, such as fresh red meat, warm milk, and strong spirituous liquors, are placed within the triangle. The necromancer stands in the south, facing the north. He speaks an invitation to the dead to come and feast on the heat and life-force of the offerings, calling them in the name and by the authority of their dark lord Nyarlathotep. If he knows the name of the shade, he voices the name repeatedly and demands the attendance of that spirit, but he may still call the dead to the circle without knowing their names, and some will come. If he knows the name of the demon he wishes to call, he voices the name of that demon.

The shades cannot leave the altar triangle. Yog-Sothoth seals shut the gates behind them. They manifest visibly either upon the air above it, or they are assisted in taking transient forms by means of rising incense smoke, or in the depths of a mirror, which the necromancer stares into after seating himself in the circle, facing the base of the altar triangle. Full manifestation of a tangible kind is rare and not to be expected. Usually the shades of the dead come as moving shadows and appear and vanish without taking on sustained, stable bodies. Yet they may be conversed with, and will answer the necromancer either in the depths of his mind or in a way that seems to the necromancer to be an ordinary voice that speaks from the very air above the triangle.

By summoning and conversing with these shades, the aspirant on this dark path learns their names and other secrets, and enlists those who are more eager and adept as his servants. In this manner his own mind is transformed by the practice of necromancy, and he is made fit to open the Lower Gate of Nyarlathotep. The night in each lunar cycle on which the ritual of opening the gate may be attempted is the night of the new moon, when the lunar orb is shrouded in darkness. The ritual is begun at midnight at the opening hour of the day of the new moon.

Success is not a matter of weeks, perhaps not even a matter of months, but may require years of dedication to the chosen way of the Crawling Chaos. As with all the disciplines of the Order, there is danger that the disciple may become so involved in the regimen itself that he forgets his higher purpose, the attainment of the black throne. Yet no seeker can become a Lord of the Order unless he has climbed the ninety-three steps of the throne mount, and entered his name in the *Necronomicon*. Only when he has received the secret mark from Nyarlathotep before the throne can he consider himself a full servant in the Work of the Trapezohedron. For then he becomes one with the purpose of the Old Ones, the restoration of the earth to the high estate from which she has fallen.

As a token of his chosen path, the child of Nyarlathotep may decide to have the seal of the dark lord tattooed on to his skin. This is not required, but is a mark of dedication to the path and respect for the lord. Whether or not the seal is adopted, the wearing of the emblem of Nyarlathotep proclaims the way walked by the disciple. It is the representation of a human skull, which may be worn as a ring, a pendant, or other forms of jewelry, or may be embroidered on to some article of clothing. The emblem should be visible to others so that they may know at a glance the disciple's preferred way of attainment.

Way of Azathoth

To walk the path of Azathoth is to become foolish in wisdom and wise in foolishness. It is the discipline that opens the Central Gate, and of all seven disciplines of the Order, is the only way that does not require Nyarlathotep as a guide. The Central Gate opens directly on the chaos throne, which lies at the center of cosmos within a great vortex of souls. These are the souls that have forgotten their names yet never received new names in the underworld, so that they merged once again into the chaos from which they were created, decayed fruit of the endlessly fertile womb of Shub-Niggurath. Many were cast into this maelstrom by Nyarlathotep, for so the Crawling Chaos deals with those who annoy him. He blasts away their flesh and their names, and consumes their souls, for his open mouth is a gateway that gapes on the black vortex.

The practice of the disciple of Azathoth is not to move in any direction, but to find the center and remain there in stillness of mind until attainment is achieved. This is the most difficult of all the seven ways, for of all things in the cosmos, none is more restless than the mind of man. The undisciplined mind is discomforted by stillness, and seeks distractions of myriad different kinds to escape from silence and inaction. It has a thousand clever tricks to avoid emptiness. Yet only by becoming mindless, like great Azathoth himself, whose true name cannot be spoken, will the disciple reach enlightenment and open the Central Gate upon the black throne.

Nyarlathotep resents those who choose to tread the way of Azathoth. Since they do not require his services as a guide to the throne, he has less opportunity to gain power over them. He does not dare to do them harm, for Azathoth feels the link with his true disciples and shields them from his messenger's wrath. Yet Nyarlathotep has scant love for those who scorn his guidance, and he always remembers their choice of path. Those who succeed in opening the Central Gate must always take upon themselves the mark of Azathoth, never the mark of Nyarlathotep, for if they receive the mark of the Crawling Chaos, they become his servants, and he will cause them to suffer for their chosen way to the throne.

For these reasons the Way of the Center is the path of the hero. It is the way of independence, the way of freedom, but also the way of peril. Those who fall from this path and fail in their discipline may know misfortune for the rest of their lives, if Nyarlathotep chooses to afflict them, and his memory is long. Those who succeed are shielded by Azathoth, whose absolute power his messenger dares not challenge. They become extensions of Azathoth, his intelligent agents, much like Nyarlathotep himself in this regard but far less potent.

The practice of those who follow the Way of the Center is to put on the yellow sash and the seal of Azathoth, and sit before the triangle altar within the circle, facing north, the spiral key of Azathoth in the triangle beside the always-wrapped Elder Seal. The disciples still their thoughts until their minds are empty. Since it is almost impossible to meditate on nothingness, they meditate on the swirling vortex of chaos. They visualize it as a great vortex of black forces rotating widdershins inwardly. At the center of this vortex they imagine the unoccupied black throne. One by one, they strip the throne of all qualities, its color, its shape, its texture, its hardness, its temperature, casting them aside until nothing remains. In this way they achieve emptiness.

The ritual of opening the Central Gate may be attempted on the night of the full moon beginning at midnight. If success is not achieved, the follower of this path may repeat the attempt on the next full moon, and so on until success is achieved. When the gate opens, the disciple of Azathoth will find himself standing before the throne. Nyarlathotep will withdraw the *Necronomicon* from beneath the throne seat and direct him to sign his name in the book beside the names of the other beings who have pledged themselves to the Work of the Trapezohedron. Then he will ask which mark the disciple shall receive, his mark or the mark of Azathoth. Followers of this path do well to choose the mark of Azathoth. Nyarlathotep will give the mark of the Nameless One who is called Azathoth, for the Crawling Chaos is his right hand.

Those who seek to fulfill this most difficult of the seven disciplines may wish to have the seal of Azathoth tattooed on their skin, as an indication to other members of the order that they have stood before the black throne and pledged their service to the great work. Or, they may choose to wear the emblem of Azathoth as a pendant, or elsewhere on their person. His emblem is a whistle, or the symbolic representation of a flute or other musical wind instrument. It is their badge of attainment, and a proclamation of their chosen path to other initiates.

It is the nature of these few that they stand apart and remain unswayed by common fears or affections. Those with the mark of Nyarlathotep are involved in the affairs of this world, but those bearing the mark of Azathoth are not of this world. They will have little direct interest in the daily affairs of the Order, and refrain from petty politics and bickering, but in times of great need may be chosen to render decisions requiring impartiality and balanced judgment. All Lords of the seven ways are equal, but the Lords of Azathoth are the foolish wise who disdain common rewards, seeking clarity and truth.

Opening the Gate

A gate is opened by Yog-Sothoth each time a spiritual creature is summoned to presence within the triangle of the altar, and each time a member of the Order projects awareness across the astral planes. All transitions through the stone circle require the opening of a gate, for no entity of spiritual substance can pass out or pass in except across a threshold, and Yog-Sothoth is the gatekeeper and holder of the keys.

The rite of Opening the Gate has a special significance. It is used to open the gate of the way chosen by a Master of the Order when he seeks to attain the black throne at the center of chaos, and thereby achieve elevation to the rank of Lord. It can only be attempted once in any cycle of the moon, and only on the lunar date devoted to the lord of that path to the throne. Yet there is no limitation on the number of times the rite may be worked by a Master seeking exploration or wisdom on the chosen path, in progress toward the ultimate objective of the black throne.

The rite of Opening the Gate differs from lesser rituals of opening in that it requires the use of the Long Chant. By the Long Chant is Nyarlathotep summoned to the stone circle in his role of psychopomp of souls. Nyarlathotep is adored as a lord of the Old Ones in other rites, but only by the voicing of the Long Chant does he attend the seeker and guide the way to the black throne.

The chaos mount is not to be attained on a single night, for the approaches are convoluted and filled with strange localities and even stranger inhabitants. Nyarlathotep reveals what must be learned to stand at last on the black steps. A little at a time he reveals it, and takes amusement in the ignorance of the seeker. He is compelled by the Long Chant and by his office as soul and messenger of the dancing gods to lead, but he is not required to make the path easy to walk. Upon each successive cycle of the moon when the gate of discipline is opened using the Long Chant, a bit more is learned that is necessary to know, until at last the throne of Azathoth is achieved.

Those who follow the way of the Central Gate do not use the Long Chant or the key of Nyarlathotep in the rite of Opening the Gate. For them there is no progress of incidents and ideas along the path, for the Central Gate opens directly at the foot of the black throne itself. They do not seek enlightenment through knowledge, but through emptiness. They emulate in their practice the idiot god, and empty their mind of all thoughts and impressions until the music of Azathoth is heard within. The sound of his flute signals the ripeness to attempt the opening of the Central Gate, which they do using only the key of Azathoth.

All other disciples employ for this rite both the key of the lord of the Old Ones who presides over their chosen path, and the key of Nyarlathotep, who is the guide along the way. A follower of the martial way of Cthulhu would use both the key of Cthulhu and the key of Nyarlathotep in opening the Gate of the South with the Long Chant. The only exception to this rule is the disciples of Nyarlathotep himself, those who follow the way of necromancy. They employ the Long Chant, but use only the key of their chosen lord, who is both their guide and their god.

The Rite of Opening

On the night of the lunar cycle appropriate for your chosen lord of the Old Ones, attend the stone circle at midnight wearing the black robe of the Order and the sash and lamen of your lord. In the triangle of the altar set the key of your lord and the key of Nyarlathotep. If your lord is Nyarlathotep, only his key will occupy the altar. If your lord is Azathoth, only his key will occupy the altar and that of Nyarlathotep will not be present. When opening the gate of any of the other five lords, both the key of that lord and the key of the Messenger are put into the altar, which also must contain the Elder Seal in its white wrapping.

Light the three flames at the points of the altar. Stand at the south of the altar triangle facing north. Empty your thoughts and still your emotions, then fill your mind with your purpose. Speak the opening words:

On this night of _____, I open the _____ Gate, in quest of the Black Throne.

There are seven possible opening statements for this rite. Which one you speak depends on which discipline you have chosen to follow for your Master work:

1. *On this night of Yig, I open the North Gate, in quest of the Black Throne.*

2. *On this night of Shub-Niggurath, I open the East Gate, in quest of the Black Throne.*

3. *On this night of Cthulhu, I open the South Gate, in quest of the Black Throne.*

4. *On this night of Dagon, I open the West Gate, in quest of the Black Throne.*

5. *On this night of Yog-Sothoth, I open the Upper Gate, in quest of the Black Throne.*

6. *On this night of Nyarlathotep, I open the Lower Gate, in quest of the Black Throne.*

7. *On this night of Azathoth, I open the Middle Gate, in quest of the Black Throne.*

Take up from the altar the key of the lord to whom the Rite of Opening is dedicated. Walk around the altar widdershins until you stand by the stone of that lord, and strike the key against the stone so that it gives off a ringing sound. Proceed around the circle, striking each stone as you pass until you return to the stone of your lord. Strike it a second time to seal the circle, and visualize a band of light of the color proper to your lord extended from stone to stone to form a heptagon. It is useful to visualize on the astral level that the astral stones are larger than the physical stones, so that the band of light cuts the air from stone to stone at the level of your heart center. Speak the words:

The circle is joined!

Proceed around the inside of the stone circle widdershins to stand before the threshold of your chosen lord. In the case of the four outer gateways you will face outward in one of the four cardinal directions, but if your lord is one of the higher lords you will stand facing inward before a threshold of the altar. Raise the rectangle of the gate from the threshold rod in your imagination, as though unrolling it upward from the rod like an inverted window shade, and visualize it standing before you like a transparent doorway. The gate has no depth, only a two-dimensional rectangular shape that is similar to a rectangle of pale light projected onto an invisible sheet of glass.

Extend your right arm and point with the key of your lord at the center of the gate. In the case of the four outer gates you point across the stone circle, breaking the plane of the circle with the key. In the case of the three inner gates, you point to the space above the altar, breaking one of the thresholds of the altar with the key. For the four lords of the other gates and for Azathoth, the key is held out straight from the body at the heart level. For Yog-Sothoth the right arm is angled upward with the key held over the altar above heart level; for Nyarlathotep the right arm is angled downward with the key held over the altar below heart level.

Press the palm of your left hand over the lamen of your lord, which hangs around your neck, and recite the following litany of opening in a clear voice if you are able to speak without being overheard by the uninitiated. Otherwise, subvocalize the words beneath your breath, speaking them clearly in your mind but not aloud on your lips.

> *In the name and by the authority of _____, great lord of the _____*
> *regions, I call upon Yog-Sothoth to open the _____ Gate upon the way to the Black*
> *Throne. Strengthen and protect me along the way, _____.*

The litany has seven forms, the choice of which is determined by the lord of your discipline:

1. *In the name and by the authority of Yig, great lord of the northern regions, I call upon Yog-Sothoth to open the North Gate upon the way to the Black Throne. Strengthen and protect me along the way, Yig.*

2. *In the name and by the authority of Shub-Niggurath, great lady of the eastern regions, I call upon Yog-Sothoth to open the East Gate upon the way to the Black Throne. Strengthen and protect me along the way, Shub-Niggurath.*

3. *In the name and by the authority of Cthulhu, great lord of the southern regions, I call upon Yog-Sothoth to open the South Gate upon the way to the Black Throne. Strengthen and protect me along the way, Cthulhu.*

4. *In the name and by the authority of Dagon, great lord of the western regions, I call upon Yog-Sothoth to open the West Gate upon the way to the Black Throne. Strengthen and protect me along the way, Dagon.*

5. *In the name and by the authority of Yog-Sothoth, great lord of the upper regions, I call upon Yog-Sothoth to open the Upper Gate upon the way to the Black Throne. Strengthen and protect me along the way, Yog-Sothoth.*

6. *In the name and by the authority of Nyarlathotep, great lord of the lower regions, I call upon Yog-Sothoth to open the Lower Gate upon the way to the Black Throne. Strengthen and protect me along the way, Nyarlathotep.*

7. *In the name and by the authority of Azathoth, great lord of the central regions, I call upon Yog-Sothoth to open the Middle Gate upon the way to the Black Throne. Strengthen and protect me along the way, Azathoth.*

Visualize on the astral level the upright rectangle of the gate opening with a spiral vortex that swirls inward in a counterclockwise direction, creating a gap or void in space above the threshold. Walk widdershins around the altar to stand in the south, facing north, and replace the key of your lord upon the altar. Take up the key of Nyarlathotep in your left hand and the Elder Seal in your right hand. Walk widdershins around the altar to stand before the opened gateway of your lord. This is the procedure for the disciples of five of the seven lords, but not for those who serve Nyarlathotep or Azathoth.

Those who serve the lord Nyarlathotep will go widdershins from the opened gate to the base of the altar and transfer the key of Nyarlathotep to their left hand, then take up the Elder Seal in their right hand and return widdershins to stand before the opened gate. Those who serve the lord Azathoth will proceed from the opened gate widdershins around the circle to the south of the altar and transfer the key of Azathoth to their left hand, taking up the Elder Seal in their right hand, then return widdershins to the opened gate.

Raise the key of Nyarlathotep in your left hand, which is the hand of reception and attraction, and point at the center of the astral vortex in the opened gate. Recite the Long Chant to call Nyarlathotep to attendance in his office of messenger of Azathoth and guide to the Black Throne. Only those who follow the path of Azathoth make no use of the Long Chant. Disciples of the other six ways must call Nyarlathotep.

Sit down before the opened gate with the Elder Seal, still wrapped in its cover, beside you on your right side and the key of Nyarlathotep (or Azathoth for the followers of Azathoth) on your left side. Open yourself to the coming of your guide, and when Nyarlathotep appears before you in the gateway, rise up in your astral body and follow him into the beginning of the path that leads to the Black Throne. Follow his steps and obey his instructions, which may be spoken or given to you in the form of silent gestures. Nyarlathotep may lead you directly to the steps of the chaos mount, but it is more probable that he will lead you only part of the way, and attempt to distract you along the path, for although he is compelled to lead those who seek the throne, he is not compelled to make the quest easy.

The disciples of Azathoth do not rely on Nyarlathotep as a guide. Their way is the most difficult, for they must find it themselves, seeking through the darkness within themselves for the center of all being. Because they make no reliance upon Nyarlathotep, the Crawling Chaos resents them and will hinder their progress if the opportunity arises.

The Elder Seal is carried in the right hand through the opened portal on the astral level, while the physical shell of the Seal remains within the stone circle, along with the physical shell of the disciple. It is to be used only at times of great danger. When unwrapped from its white covering, it will banish whatever evil threatens along the path, and will cast the seeker back into his physical body with a forceful reaction. It also sends Nyarlathotep away, so that his guidance is lost until the next attempt is made to reach the black throne.

Do not uncover the Elder Seal except in the most dire need, for all creatures on the path to the throne resent its use and will be more obstructive on the next attempt. This is also true of Nyarlathotep himself, who cannot bear the exposure of the Seal for more than a few moments, but must withdraw when it is uncovered. He views it as an affront that the Seal should be uncovered in his presence, and his memory is long in malice.

After the attempt to reach the throne has either been successful or has failed, arise and carry the key and Seal widdershins to the southern side of the altar, then place them back on the altar. Take up the key of your lord in your right hand (or if you are a follower of Azathoth or Nyarlathotep, transfer the key to your right hand) and go widdershins back to the stone of your lord. Strike the key on the stone. Speak the words:

The circle is broken!

Visualize on the astral level the colored light that links the seven stones flicker and vanish. Go widdershins around to the south of the altar and stand before the base of the triangle, facing north. This is both your starting and ending posture for all rites. Replace the key of your lord upon the altar, then stand quietly for a minute or two to clear your mind. Extinguish the three altar lights and take off your lamen and sash to formally end the rite.

Approaching the Throne

When the Long Chant is uttered during the Opening of the Gate, Nyarlathotep will come to the portal and stand upon the far side of the vortex. Those who are skilled in astral travel, such as the disciples of the way of Yog-Sothoth, will see him in one of his familiar guises. Commonly he appears dressed in the black robes of a Bedouin with his face veiled, yet sometimes he adopts the form of a golden-skinned prince of Egypt. He comes only to those who are ready to begin the quest for the black throne, and to them he extends his hand. Do not take his hand, or touch him in any way, but follow him. Those who are not prepared for the astral planes he ignores, no matter how often they petition him.

Only Masters of the Order well skilled in second sight and the projection of the subtle husk will see Nyarlathotep with their inner vision. Other disciples may fail to see him, but may sense his unseen presence, or hear his words inwardly, or feel his chill breath. Not every member of the Order is equally skilled in astral perception. It is usually those who follow the way of Yog-Sothoth who are most gifted with the sight, as should be so—for those with astral gifts should pursue the way of Yog-Sothoth, those with martial gifts should follow Cthulhu, those naturally fitted for scholarly study should apprentice themselves to Dagon, sensualists and lovers of beauty and art should follow Shub-Niggurath, those concerned with the health, fitness, and grace of the body should follow Yig, and those rare few who seek unattachment from all earthly things should walk the path of Azathoth.

It seldom happens that the messenger of the dancing gods will lead the seeker directly to the lowermost step of the throne mount. He is tasked to bring to the throne only those worthy to have their names inscribed in the black book beneath it. More often he escorts the seeker across the astral planes to a scene that contains teachings that will advance the quest. The disciple must remain open to all impressions received while in the astral shell, and must strive to remember them. When he returns to the stone circle and to his physical body, he is advised to write down all that he has seen and heard, so that it will not be forgotten. Even the most trivial event may have significance at later stages in the quest for the throne.

Those who tread one of the paths of the six lesser lords will be confronted and challenged by astral creatures who seek to test their courage and dedication. These horrifying beings must be faced without doubt in the heart, for the least uncertainty is a flaw that may shatter the resolve of the seeker. Use the Elder Sign with the right hand to dispel these creatures of nightmare.

The way of its making is this: touch the tip of the index finger to the tip of the thumb, cross the middle finger over the top of the ring finger, and raise the small finger upward. The Elder Sign is also useful to test the truthfulness of entities and scenes along the path. If they are intended to ensnare and delude, the Elder Sign will reveal this falsehood. The Elder Sign is less powerful than the Elder Seal. Do not uncover the Seal except in the gravest peril. In most averse circumstances the Elder Sign will suffice.

In the fullness of time, an accomplished Master of the Order who has devoted all his will and talents to the quest will be led to the throne mount. The stone portal of Yog-Sothoth remains open behind him when he has passed through its pointed arch, and leads directly back to the stone circle, for he is given one final opportunity to renounce the quest. Should he falter in his resolve and escape backward through the portal, Nyarlathotep will never come again in the guise of messenger. The Work of the Trapezohedron is not for the faint of heart, but only for those who recognize the ultimate futility of mortal existence, which is a bondage of the spirit in chains of flesh.

At the foot of the ninety-three steps are two black hounds, each as large as a small horse, with great heads filled with gleaming white teeth and black eyes that glow red in their depths with hellfire. These are hounds of Tindalos who serve Azathoth, even in his madness. Their dog-like shape is only a veil, not a true representation of their appearance, as indeed all things seen on the chaos mount are merely veils, for the realities would blast the human mind to cinders. Each is chained into place, but the length of the chains permits the dogs to guard the ascent to the throne.

To pass these tireless sentinels, show the Elder Seal wrapped in its white linen, and hold it up before you. Do not unwrap it, for if you expose the Seal, the chaos mount will vanish and you will find yourself once more within your own seated body. As you pass between the hounds, keep your hand upon the tie that binds the Seal. The dogs will withdraw grudgingly and let you ascend, but if for any reason they smell fear or deceit upon you, they will lunge against their chains, and then you must save yourself by exposing the Elder Seal, if you can.

For some, the steps will seem fewer than their number, but for others they multiply themselves in their myriads so that the ascent to the throne appears endless. All the while, the black vortex of chaos whirls like a great wheel around the throne mount, filled with the wailing of lost souls that rises above the piping of Azathoth's flute. As you approach the summit, the ring of the dancing gods defines itself against the rushing blackness, resembling a pale halo of gigantic, translucent figures about the triple throne. Some are human, but the others are monstrous and strange. All are blind, all imperfect in some part of their bodies, for they were obedient to the will of Azathoth, and only Nyarlathotep defied him. They move around the throne more slowly than the vortex of chaos, and in the opposite direction, for whereas the vortex turns widdershins around the throne mount, the gods dance sunwise, as though dancing against the pressure of a black, invisible wind.

Azathoth sprawls naked upon his throne, mired in his own filth, his matted hair hanging over the empty sockets of his eyes, his cracked flute of bone pressed to his fat lips, his fingers moving deftly across the sound holes in a pattern so complex that it appears random. At his feet lies his golden crown, where it was cast from his head. It lies misshapen but not broken. On the empty seat at his right-hand side is the iron crown of the prince foretold in destiny, which Nyarlathotep puts on but cannot yet claim as his own. On the empty seat at his left-hand side, the silver crown of his daughter Barbelzoa sits, where the shining goddess left it before plunging into the pit of stars.

Stand before the throne and speak your petition to Azathoth in these words:

Great Azathoth, creator and destroyer of worlds, whose true name must never be spoken, the beginning and the end, lord of chaos, hear my declaration of service. I voluntarily take upon myself the noble and great Work of the Trapezohedron, and swear to strive for its fulfillment all

the days of my life, to keep the work secret from the uninitiated and profane, and to combat
any and all who seek to oppose the perfection of the great Work. These things I swear with my
true name and with my blood.

Nyarlathotep will withdraw from beneath the black throne the *Necronomicon*. All who see the book see it in a different form. To some it is a black tome of heavy leather bindings, to others a black scroll on a roller of bone and silver, to yet others a set of clay tablets. The god will lay it open so that it floats upon the air before you, and now is your opportunity to turn its pages and study its secrets. The progress of time at the chaos mount is not as the progress of time in the lower world. You may read much if you choose, but never forget your primary purpose, lest Nyarlathotep grow impatient and, with a lash of his hand, send you flying backward down the steps and through the gate of Yog-Sothoth.

The messenger of Azathoth will show you the place to sign your name and give you a reed with which to prick your left hand and draw your blood. This should be understood in an astral sense, for the blood of the physical body is not drawn or shed during this rite. With this reed you must sign your true name in the book. The true name is the name given to you by your parent or parents, or the first name given to you by those with authority over you if by chance you were abandoned at birth. The true name is not yours to choose, but is the name chosen for you by another before you had the power of choice.

When you have signed, Nyarlathotep will ask you in words or by gestures if you agree to receive his mark upon your skin. Those who follow the path of Azathoth should deny him, and demand the mark of Azathoth. This will displease the Crawling Chaos, but he cannot refuse. He will act in the place of Azathoth and use the nail of one finger to mark you upon the astral body. The disciples of the six lesser lords must make the difficult decision whether to accept the mark of Nyarlathotep, or defy him and take the mark of Azathoth. Most would do well to accept the mark of the Crawling Chaos, for this acquiescence turns aside his ire.

When you pass through the gate of Yog-Sothoth at the foot of the chaos mount, and find yourself once more in your body, end the ritual of Opening the Way and strip yourself naked. Search your body will diligence, and you will find a scar or blemish that you have not previously seen. This is the mark of Nyarlathotep or Azathoth, which binds you to your oath in this world, as your name inscribed in the *Necronomicon* binds you to your obligation in the higher worlds.

Rite of the Dancing Gods

The solemn rite of the dancing gods takes place on two dates of the yearly cycle, when the periods of day and night are equal and stand in balance. On these dates the barriers between this world and the higher worlds are thin, and the gate of Yog-Sothoth is easily opened. As the head and tail of the dragon are to the monthly cycle of the moon, so the equinoxes are to the yearly cycle of the sun. They are dates of transition and passage. Great works of magic may be accomplished on these two dates, baneful works on the equinox that heralds the approach of winter, but beneficent works on the equinox that ushers in the summer.

The dancing gods manifest the creative will of Azathoth that is expressed through the intervals of sound and silence in his music. Their ceaseless dance frames the laws of the cosmos, both the laws that bring forth, and the laws that annihilate. They possess no free will of their own, but only act in accordance with his will. Yet his will is individualized through them, giving them the semblance of choice. Before the tragic ending of the last age, they danced in joy that mirrored the joy of Azathoth, but now they dance in sorrow that mirrors his sorrow, blind and mindless, as is their lord.

They may be petitioned by rituals, each individually in his or her designated sphere of works, which is defined in part by the sign of the zodiac associated with each god. Even though they have no separate will, because they represent facets of the unconscious will of Azathoth, the twelve parts of his divided will can be ritually invoked and turned to uses that fall under their categories. Be aware that the responses of the dancing gods are capricious, for they are all insane, as is their lord.

The rite of the dancing gods honors all twelve who remain—once there were thirteen, and now there are twelve. This mystery is expressed in the number of months in the year. In some reckonings there are thirteen months that are based on the thirteen yearly cycles of the moon, but in other reckonings there are twelve months marked by the progress of the sun through the heavens. The descent of the apostate Nyarlathotep wrought this transformation on the cosmos, but some cults of the goddess Barbelzoa remember the thirteen in their perfection before her fall from grace.

As many as seven may work the rite within the stone circle. Others of the Order who gather to observe this rite should seat themselves between the stones, or beyond the stones in the quarter of their choice. The rite may also be worked by a solitary initiate or self-initiate of the Order of the Old Ones, of any rank, in the circle. It is a rite of honoring and praise, which attracts the sleeping awareness of the dancing gods and inclines them to favor the magician and his purposes. It creates a sympathetic link between the dancing gods, who order the events of the universe, and those who perform the rite. The practical consequence is good fortune in daily life.

Set the twelve seals of the dancing gods in a circle within the altar triangle, in the order of the zodiac signs, but reversed, as if the circle of the zodiac had been brought down from heaven and laid upon the ground. It is oriented with Aries (Athoth) in the east, followed in a clockwise circle by Taurus (Harmas), Gemini (Galila), Cancer (Yobel) in the south, Leo (Adonaios), Virgo (Cain), Libra (Abel) in the west, Scorpio (Akiressina), Sagittarius (Yubel), Capricorn (Harmupiael) in the north, Aquarius (Archiradonin), and Pisces (Belias).

In the center of the circle of twelve seals, place the key of Nyarlathotep, who is the soul and messenger of the dancing gods, as well as of Azathoth, for the dancing gods are extensions of Azathoth, as is Nyarlathotep himself. Inside the upper point of the altar triangle put the Elder Seal, so that it is inside the triangle but outside the circle of the dancing gods. Wear the seal of Nyarlathotep around your neck, and the orange sash of Nyarlathotep at the waist of your black robe. The exception to this rule are those Lords who have received the mark of Azathoth upon their astral bodies at the chaos mount—they should wear the seal and sash of Azathoth to show their allegiance to him.

Light the three altar flames so that its triangular boundary is actualized on the astral level. Stand in the south at the base of the altar, facing north—the starting position for all rituals within the stone circle. Speak the opening words, or if you work the ritual where you may be overhead by the uninitiated, subvocalize them in your throat:

> On this vernal [or autumnal] equinox, when day and night are equal, and cosmos and chaos stand in balance, I honor the twelve dancing gods who order and regulate all earthly events.

When the rite is conducted on the night of the spring equinox you use the words "vernal equinox," and when the rite is conducted on the night of the fall equinox you use the words "autumnal equinox."

Take up the key of Nyarlathotep and walk around the altar widdershins until you stand before the orange stone of Nyarlathotep. Strike the stone gently with the key so that the key gives forth a ringing tone. Continue around the circle counterclockwise in a complete circle, striking each stone as you pass it, until you have returned to the stone of Nyarlathotep. Strike the orange stone a second time to join the end of the circle with its beginning on the astral level. Speak the words:

> The circle is joined!

Visualize orange rays of astral light linking the stones of the circle, so that the stones stand at the points of a heptagon. Return widdershins to stand at the south of the altar, and replace the key of Nyarlathotep in the center of the triangle.

Take up the seal of Adonaios, which is linked with the zodiac sign Leo and with the sun. Carry it widdershins to the yellow stone of Azathoth. Touch the seal to the stone to establish the link between Adonaios and the lord Azathoth, who rules over him. Carry the seal of Adonaios widdershins to the gate of Azathoth, which is the yellow rod on the right side of the altar triangle. Extend the seal in your hand across the threshold of the yellow rod, holding it over the center of the altar at the level of your heart. Speak the words of praise:

Adonaios, I honor you and praise your works in the name of Azathoth, your ruling lord.
Look with favor upon this circle, and confer good fortune upon those who serve the will of
Nyarlathotep, your soul and messenger.

Touch the seal disk of Adonaios to your forehead, kiss the disk on its rim, and press it over your heart center beneath your folded hands. Visualize a yellow light glowing in the air above the altar that is similar in color to the rim of the seal disk of the god. It is the color associated with Azathoth. Let it shine outward so that it fills the stone circle with gentle light. The light of lord Azathoth carries the blessing of Adonaios into the circle, so that it falls upon the heads of those who stand within its boundary.

Walk around the circle widdershins to stand in the south, and return the seal disk of the god Adonaios to its place within the altar triangle. If you perform this rite alone, take up the disk of the god Yobel, and perform the same series of actions in honor and praise of Yobel that you performed in honor of Adonaios. The words of praise addressed to each god are the same, save only that the name of the ruling lord is changed. The disks are taken up in an ordering that defines the solar and lunar sects of the zodiac signs. The correct sequence by which the gods are praised is listed below.

    Adonaios (Leo): "name of Azathoth" (Sun)
    Yobel (Cancer): "name of Dagon" (Moon)
    Cain (Virgo): "name of Nyarlathotep" (Mercury)
    Galila (Gemini): "name of Nyarlathotep" (Mercury)
    Abel (Libra): "name of Shub-Niggurath" (Venus)
    Harmas (Taurus): "name of Shub-Niggurath" (Venus)
    Akiressina (Scorpio): "name of Cthulhu" (Mars)
    Athoth (Aries): "name of Cthulhu" (Mars)
    Yubel (Sagittarius): "name of Yog-Sothoth" (Jupiter)
    Belias (Pisces): "name of Yog-Sothoth" (Jupiter)
    Harmupiael (Capricorn): "name of Yig" (Saturn)
    Archiradonin (Aquarius): "name of Yig" (Saturn)

If you work the Rite of the Dancing Gods with another initiate, you will alternate in praising the gods, first taking up a disk and speaking the words of praise, then allowing your companion to take up the next disk and speak the words of praise, and so to the last of the twelve disks. If more than two conduct the rite within the circle, each shall in turn take up a disk and speak the words, and all shall visualize the color of light of the god's lord filling the circle, as indicated by the coloring of the rim of the seal disk.

All circumambulation around the altar is widdershins. Those working the rite shall space themselves equally around the circle—if two, the leader of the rite shall stand to the south of the altar in the starting position, and the companion shall stand opposite in the north, and shall preserve this distance whenever there is the requirement to walk about the altar. When it is the turn of the companion to take up a disk, the leader of the rite, who began it with the first disk, shall stand opposite in the north when the companion takes up the next disk from the south.

When a god is praised who is linked to one of the lords of the inner gates, the seal disk of that god is extended above the altar; but when a god is praised who is linked to one of the lords of the outer gates, the seal disk is extended beyond the stone circle in the direction of that outer gate, even as is done in the worship of the seven lords during the daily rites. Through the seven gates of the lords are the blind forces of the twelve dancing gods invoked, each through his or her particular gate.

The Long Chant

1

O-do bu-ta-mo-na ki-ka-le

(Odo butmona cicle)

Be opened, the mouth of mystery.

2

U-me-di u-pa-ah-he zod-on-gu

(Umd upaah zong)

Be called, the wings of the winds.

3

Zod-am-ran i-al-per-e-ji

(Zamran ialprg)

Appear, the burning flames,

4

I-zoda-zoda-zod pi-ad-pa-be

(Izazaz piadph)

Framed in the depths of my jaws.

5

No-quod-i Ya-i-da

(Noquodi Iaida)

You servants of the Highest,

6

Panu-pi-re mala-pi-re-ji

(Panpir malpirgi)

Pour down your living fire;

7

Vau-nigi-laji o-de im-u-a-mar-e

(Uniglag od imvamar)

Descend and manifest

8

Mi-cala-zod-o i-oi ko-me-sala-be

(Micalzo ioi comselh)

Your power in this circle,

9

O-de i-oi o-re-ri

(Od ioi orri)

And in these stones,

10

O-de i-oi pi-re di

(Od ioi pire d)

And in this holy triangle.

11

O-zoda-zod-ama ji-vi i-zodi-zod-o-pe

(Ozazm givi izizop)

Make of me a mighty vessel

12

O-ma o-de va-o-anu

(Oma od vaoan)

Of understanding and truth,

13

Di-es ar-jide-ko

(Ds argedco)

Who invokes

14

Do-o-ai-pe qo-a-ala ma-da

(Dooaip qaal mad)

In the name of the creator

15

Te-lo-ka vo-vi-me

(Teloc vovim)

Him that is fallen,

16

Bala-zoda-reji do-si-ji oxi-ai-ala

(Balzarg dosig oxiayal)

Steward of the dark throne.

17

Yiii-eee! Nyar-lath-o-tep!

(Iä! Nyarlathotep!)

Hail! Nyarlathotep!

18
Ka-na-le A-za-thoth
(Canal Azathoth)
Artisan of Azathoth,

19
Dari-lapi o-sa o-de go-he-da
(Drilpi os od gohed)
Greatest of the twelve and one

20
Di-es ka-he-sa o-sa kala-zoda
(Ds chis os calz)
Who are twelve in the firmament.

21
Tore-zod-u o-de zod-am-er-an
(Torzu od zamran)
Arise and show yourself!

22
O-la sura-zod-asa a-da-na
(Ol surzas adna)
I swear obedience

23
Da-e dar-i-lapa ba-be
(De drilpa bab)
To the great work,

24
Ma-da yada-na-he ka-hil-da-o
(Mad iadnah childao)
Divine jewel of knowledge,

25
A-zodia-ji-ere kon-jame-pebe-la-jab
(Aziagiar congamphlgh)
The harvest of human souls;

26
A-re ba-ba-lonu
(Ar babalon)
To winnow the wicked;

27
Fi-fala-zoda lev-itab-monji
(Fifalz levithmong)
To root out the beasts;

28
Vi-ru-den o-ar
(Viruden or)
To beautify the ground.

29
Di-es para-di-zoda pa-sa-ba-sa
(Ds paradiz pasbs)
That virgin daughter

30
No-an ba-ba-lon-da
(Noan babalond)
Become a harlot,

31
Er-em ta-tab-en
(Erm tatan)
Ark of wormwood,

32

Zod-on-ak pa-tara-lax ob-de mo-ma

(Zonac patralx od mom)

Clothed in rock and moss:

33

Go-ho-lor ti-la-ba

(Goholor tilb)

To lift her up,

34

A-oi-ve-ai ma-ho-rel-a

(Aoiveae mahorela)

Star in the dark heavens,

35

Ex-en-tas-er lu-kif-ti-as

(Exentaser luciftias)

Mother of all brightness;

36

O-ah-li ti-la-ba ox-i-ay-al

(Oali tilb oxiayal)

To place her on the mighty seat,

37

Vi-vau e-la

(Viu el)

Second of the first.

38

O-le i-mu-a-mar

(Ol imvamar)

I dedicate myself

39

Fi-fi-sa oi vau-nu

(Fifis oi vaun)

To carry out this work

40

O-la doo-ai-nu o-da ka-ni-la

(Ol dooain od cnila)

By my name and blood.

41

Bo-la-pe zod-or-ji

(Bolp zorge)

Be you friendly to me;

42

Zod-ir-do no-ko ma-da

(Zirdo noco mad)

I am the servant of the same god as you,

43

Ho-a-tha-he Ya-i-da

(Hoath Iaida)

True worshipper of the Highest;

44

El-a-pe zod-ir yo-i-ada

(Lap zir ioiad)

For I am of him that lives forever.

This incantation, known as the Long Chant, is in the language of the Enochian angels, as delivered to John Dee, who is said by some to have made translation of the *Necronomicon* for his own study. Its use is the calling forth of Nyarlathotep and the servants of Azathoth known as the Old Ones through the gates of Yog-Sothoth to the stone circle. Yog-Sothoth is not called, but others are called through his gates, and in the opening of the gates Yog-Sothoth is manifested. The chant may be used to open the six ways of the six directions to the black throne, but not the seventh way of the center, which is opened by silence. The Long Chant also serves to open the way of any working of magic in accord with the will of Azathoth.

Each line of the chant is printed here in three forms, first in the Enochian language as it is to be intoned on the breath, second as the Enochian words were penned on paper by John Dee, and third in translation as spoken in the common tongue. Each line should be voiced first in Enochian, and then in English. The second version of each line is not to be uttered, but shows the correct writing of the Enochian text.

If the disciple who seeks the black throne is so fortunate as to have a partner in the rite, each line of the chant is intoned by both, first by the seeker in Enochian, and second by the helper in the rite in English. In this way a rhythmic chant is made back and forth across the circle from one to the other. If the seeker works the rite alone, he must voice both forms of each line, first in Enochian and then in English.

The spoken form of the Enochian lines of the chant may appear strange and uncouth to the eye, but there is purpose in its structure, for in the Enochian language, each separate letter is a living spirit, and must be noticed on the breath when speaking Enochian words, in order that its power shall become actualized. Only when it is voiced aloud does the spirit of an Enochian letter acquire being in this realm of reality, and is then able to express its force in the world. Unspoken, it remains uncreated. It is for this reason that Enochian words contain no silent letters, but each letter contributes a part of the sound of the word, be it ever so small a part.